Roadburg, Alan
Life After Teaching

ISBN 0-9730027-2-7

1. Retirement - Lifestyle, non-financial. 2. Teachers.
3. Self-help
I. Title

Second Career Program, 2900 Steeles Ave. E., Suite 216, Thornhill ON L3T 4X1

This book may be customized and purchased in quantities. For details contact the Sales Department at the above address, email admin@afterteaching.com, or call 1-800-445-3360

Printed and bound in The United States

Contents

Ken Swanson, President
Illinois Education Association

Dear IEA Colleague:

Although retirement may not be the most important issue facing you today, preparing for retirement is much more than having enough years of service credit and completing the correct retirement forms. Retiring involves an understanding of how to transition from a very complex and high-energy profession to a life with much less structure, no bells and much less mayhem. Most school employees look forward to and embrace retirement with much success. They had a plan.

However, many of my colleagues who have retired have expressed to me a genuine sense of loss. Even though their career had presented many aggravations, they had forgotten that it also was a source of satisfaction and self-esteem and they had not created a plan to replace those necessary nutrients of life.

I am very pleased that the Illinois Education Association Retired has developed a relationship with Dr. Alan Roadburg and are able to share with you his publication Life After Teaching: Road Map To Retirement Happiness. I have enjoyed this book and I recommend it to you. I also hope that it will provide you with many good ideas as to how to prepare for retirement. It has helped me to recognize that my retirement road map is still under construction and that it is not too soon to start building those bridges.

Ken Swanson

Ken Swanson

"If situations are defined as real,
they are real in their consequences."
(W.I. Thomas, 1923)

OTHER BOOKS BY ALAN ROADBURG, Ph.D.

Re-tire With A Dash
What Are You Doing After Work?
A Retirement Lifestyle Planning Guide For Financial Advisors

INTRODUCTION

This book was written specifically for teachers who are either contemplating retirement or have recently retired. *Life After Teaching* is based on two irrefutable facts: (1) Money alone will not guarantee retirement happiness. Money helps, but you will be spending both time and money in retirement and the key to retirement happiness can be found in lifestyle. (2) Although teachers share many elements of the retirement experience with others, some of their experiences, interests, viewpoints, and perceptions differ from those in other occupations. As such, planning for a life after teaching requires additional considerations and insight.

Retirement today must reflect the needs and circumstances of an emerging new breed of retirees, the Baby Boomers. The Boomers will live longer, retire richer, are more highly educated, and expect more from life compared to any group of retirees in the past. The standard approach to retirement lifestyle planning, including the image of retirement itself, has not kept up-to-date with these changes. The outdated approach often includes value judgments and issues that relate more to ageing than to retirement.

We look upon retirement as a journey through an unknown area and our objective is to provide you with a road map to ensure that your retirement will be worthwhile and enjoyable. Why is a road map necessary? Keep in mind that retirement is a unique experience that will not reveal its true identity until after you actually retire. No matter how much planning you do, conditions may change. Your retirement may be completely different from what you imagined before you retired. Because you won't know what your retirement will be like until you retire, this book will provide you with 'Life Goal Planning' tools and techniques to guide you and ensure that your retirement will be worthwhile, enjoyable and purposeful.

Most people understand the importance of planning financially for retirement and do not leave this up to chance. The problem is the non-financial side of retirement planning - lifestyle planning – is often left up to chance. Based on my extensive experience delivering retirement planning workshop for thousands of pre- and post-retirees, two-thirds of pre-retirees do not have concrete future retirement plans. This book addresses this issue head-on, by providing you with direction to create or perhaps improve your retirement plans before or after you retire.

As your road map to retirement happiness, *Life After Teaching* includes two valuable and unique components – Life Goal Planning instructions on how to guide your retirement career so that it will be worthwhile and enjoyable, plus the experiences and advice of retired teachers.

The Life Goal Planning component is based on over 20 years experience (academic and practical) conducting hundreds of retirement lifestyle workshops. You will find a simple step-by-step proven method to ensure that satisfactions lost from work will be replaced in retirement.

This book also includes the results of an exclusive online survey among Retired Teachers. Recognizing the tremendous benefits to be gained through the experiences of retired teachers, we designed an online survey to enable your retired colleagues to act as 'retirement mentors'. This research was conducted specifically for this book and the survey results are presented in the appropriate chapters throughout the book.

To initiate the research, we contacted a number of retired teachers'associations asking if they could direct their members to our online survey Web site. The questionnaire focused on their experience planning for and in retirement, including their impressions of the main benefits and drawbacks of retirement. They were also asked what advice they would provide for teachers contemplating retirement. This unique research can be an invaluable resource from your peers who 'have been there'.[1]

In addition to Life Goal Planning tools and the Retired Teachers Online Survey results, I present an entirely new way of looking at retirement that reflects the needs and concerns of today's retirees. To differentiate the new retirement from retirement in the past, I introduce the concept of 're-tire with a dash'. To retire (without the dash) refers to giving up work - the outdated image of retirement from the past - while re-tire (with a dash) refers to finding activities that are worthwhile and enjoyable.

---

1. An online survey is not a representative sample, it can have limitations. There is a likelihood that only those people who are motivated to speak out will take the time to complete a survey. Nevertheless, we ended up with a broad range of teacher respondents and collected a snapshot of their retirement situation, plus a wealth of information, advice, and impressions. You will find this to be a unique and valuable resource in planning your own retirement.

I use the technique of an ongoing character dialogue to illustrate the key points of Life Goal Planning. The dialogues are not intended to reflect the life experiences of all teachers but will illustrate the key points to the reader in an enjoyable way. While the characters you will meet are fictional, the issues, theories, ideas, concepts, and examples that we discuss are based on the real life experiences of various participants in my retirement workshops and discussions with teachers who are recently retired or considering retirement. The results of the retired teachers' research is integrated with the character dialogue and presented at the appropriate point.

Chapter 1 *(Handyman)* introduces a new way to look at retirement - 're-tire with a dash'. This chapter outlines what retirement is or can be today, rather than what it was in the past. The Baby Boomers will face a new retirement requiring a new perspective and updated guidelines.

Chapter 2 *(Do You Want to Know A Secret?)* reveals the secret to retirement happiness based on how you will spend your time in retirement.

Chapter 3 *(Ticket To Ride)* is an overview of the Life Goal Planning Workshop - a unique process that will teach you how to guide your retirement career so that it will be worthwhile and enjoyable. You will learn how to evaluate your retirement plans, maybe improve them, and how to develop new ideas should you need them.

Chapter 4 (*You Can't Always Get What You Want*) addresses the issue of what happens if you know what you want to do in re-tirement but for some reason you can't do it. You will learn that you have an 'ace up your sleeve'.

Chapter 5 (*A Hard Day's Night*) looks at working after retirement. I present several issues to consider including the question, "Are you taking the easy way out?"

Chapter 6 *(Money... Can't Buy Me Love)* integrates lifestyle planning with financial planning. A financial plan is based on a financial goal, which in turn is based on future lifestyle plans. Life Goal Planning is the missing element in retirement planning.

Chapter 7 *(Did You Ever Have To Make Up Your Mind?)* helps with the decision to retire. You will learn techniques to turn an otherwise subjective decision into an objective one.

Chapter 8 *(When I'm Sixty-Four)* responds to a question raised by The Beatles over 40 years ago. I present an entirely different way of looking at ageing and argue that it has absolutely nothing to do with retirement.

Chapter 9 *(With A Little Help From My Friends)* focuses on relationships in retirement. It includes real life examples of problems that can emerge, and offers suggestions on how to deal with them. Because not everyone is married at retirement, we also look at friendships.

Chapter 10 *(Our House)* focuses on moving after retirement. We look at some potential problems and how to overcome them. What happens if you want to move but your partner doesn't? Or, you move and later realize you made a mistake?

Chapter 11 (*Go Where You Wanna Go*) includes the results of the retired teachers' online survey that pertain to the advantages, drawbacks, and advice presented by your retired colleagues with respect to preparing for retirement.

Chapter 12 (*Imagine*) includes the summary.

Part 2 includes step-by-step instructions to complete the Life Goal Planning Workshop either on your own or with a small group of friends, colleagues, or relatives. This workshop is based on over 20 years experience (academic and practical) conducting hundreds of retirement lifestyle workshops. You will find a simple proven method to ensure that satisfactions lost from teaching will be replaced in retirement.

You may notice that several issues that typically appear in other retirement (without the dash) lifestyle books and courses have been excluded or dealt with in a new way. Issues such as health, end of life resources, social services, and retirement communities are purposely excluded. Granted, these can be important and they can be found in other books. But since they have nothing to do with the transition from a work to a retirement career, they do not appear in this book.

Because my expertise lies with the non-financial side of retirement planning, this book will not increase your nest egg or reduce taxes. But having worked alongside many financial planning professionals over the years running workshops, I recognize the importance of combining financial and life goal planning and hence the development of this program and dedicated book, *Life After Teaching*. In the following pages, I have distilled my more than 20 years of academic and practical experience into a simple program that will lead you step by step through your retirement career so that you can optimize the probability that your retirement will be worthwhile and enjoyable.

No matter who you are, retired or not, or whether or not you have plans, if you want to 're-tire' with a dash and learn the secret to retirement happiness, this book is for you. The secret is very simple, easy to implement, and as you will discover, quite obvious.

Now let's discover how to 're-tire' with a dash!

Retired Teachers Research Results

One of the most important sources for help, guidance and advice on life after teaching is the experiences and advice of your retired colleagues. Even though each person's retirement experience is unique, you can still benefit from the experiences of others, especially those who share your professional background.

To tap this important source, we set up an online survey and recruited retired teachers in the United States and Canada. We asked representatives of a number of retired teachers' associations to let their members know that we were conducting research on retirement through an online Web site. We were very pleased with the response especially because the research was carried out during the summer when most people are on holidays.

I refer to the subjects of this research as 'Retirement Mentors'. A mentor is defined as "a wise and trusted counselor or teacher", and a retirement mentor is in a sense an experienced retiree. He or she has been there and is willing to share their experiences and advice for your benefit. To my knowledge this is the only current research of this type among teachers, and needless to say, it can be extremely valuable for your future retirement. There are no rehearsals for retirement, so you would be wise to learn from your retired colleagues experiences.

I acknowledge the limitations of this type of research. It is possible that those people who feel strongly for or against an issue may be more likely to take the time to respond. Also, because the research took place online through a Web site, we were excluding those people who did not have Internet access. Nevertheless, we were pleased with the response rate and the range of responses. I believe we ended up with a fairly representative sample that accurately reflects the valuable experiences and opinions of retired teachers.

In addition to basic demographic information, we looked into the factors influencing the decision to retire, type and degree of retirement education or preparation, activities in retirement including work and voluntary activities, moving after retirement, and overall satisfaction in retirement. The respondents were also presented with open-ended questions where they could express their opinions freely on the main attractions and drawbacks of retirement. Lastly, they were asked what advice they would give to other teachers contemplating retirement. Like most things in life, views on retirement differ. The results of this research will be presented at the approprite section throughout the book to assist you with your life after teaching. We start with the subject characteristics. (NOTE: Totals from those questions that encourage multiple responses may exceed 100%)

Respondent Demographics

Sample Size: 450

Gender

Female	66%
Male	33%

Current Age

<60	31%
61-64	26%
65-69	21%
> 70	22%

(Continued)

Age at Retirement from Teaching

< 60	70%
60-62	16%
63-64	4%
65	4%
66-69	3%
> 70	3%

Type of Work Before Retirement

Elementary Teaching	44%
Secondary Teaching	34%
College/University Teaching	6%
Administration	16%

Marital Status

Married	77%
Widowed	7%
Never married	7%
Separated/divorced	9%

Health Status

Excellent	26%
Very good	45%
Good	26%
Poor	3%

As you can see, our sample represents the general teacher population. It is interesting to note that 90% of our subjects retired before age 65. We will look into their reasons for retiring and many other interesting issues in due course.

1

Handyman

(*James Taylor, 1977*)

I'm a bit of a handyman and I enjoy doing odd jobs around the house. One sunny day a few weeks ago I was working on my fence when my neighbour Dave poked his head over.

"Hi neighbour," he said. "Working hard?"

"Not too big a job," I replied. "Once I fix this post I'm going to paint the fence."

"I'll help you paint!" he said with a smile.

Dave's offer was a bit unusual. I could tell he had something on his mind. Dave and his wife Diane had been good neighbors over the years; we didn't see each other socially, but often chatted as we did yard work and had a friendly arrangement of loaning tools. I accepted his offer and said I would be ready in about an hour.

True to his word Dave appeared dressed in his working clothes with a paintbrush and stool in hand. I couldn't help thinking about Tom Sawyer and how he convinced others to paint Aunt Polly's fence. The difference was Tom and his friends had one brush between them so Tom rested while others painted. Dave had the foresight to bring his own brush.

We worked quietly for a few minutes and then he said, "I've been wondering. I know you work with retirees and we have a bit of a problem. Diane suggested I talk to you; she thought maybe you could help."

Dave is as a teacher and his wife Diane is in pharmaceutical sales. A while ago he mentioned he was starting to think about retiring and I had a pretty good idea he had some concerns about this.

"What's the problem?" I asked.

"We talked about this before," he said, "but lately I have been thinking about retiring and last week Diane and I went to a retirement seminar put on by her company. It was quite, how should I put this, an eye-opener."

"In what way?" I replied.

"Well mostly it was good, but I can't help feeling sort of scared. I have been working for more than thirty years and I like teaching. I don't know if scared is the right word, but I am feeling uncertain about the future. I don't have to retire now, and some of my buddies kid me and say I would be a fool not to retire. The problem is, I really don't know what to do."

"What about some of your friends who are retired?" I asked. "How is it working out for them?"

"Well, my friend Les is an accountant and he retired about a year ago. I think he's having real problems - not money problems though. When he first retired he kept telling me how busy he was. But after a while it seems he ran out of things to do. In fact he got quite depressed. I haven't seen him for a while and the last thing I want is to be like him with everyone feeling sorry for me."

To shift Dave's focus away from one bad example and

to start him thinking about retirement in a more positive way, I said, "I can understand your concern, Dave. After all, retiring involves major changes in your life. The problem is we are trained and educated for most things in life, except retirement."

"That is so true," he replied. "I was hoping that the seminar would help, but it didn't. I have spoken to a few retired teachers I know but I seem to be getting mixed messages. Some are having a great time, while others; well let's just say they miss teaching. I have done some reading on retirement, but I'm confused."

"Why don't you tell me about the seminar you and Diane attended?" I suggested.

As Dave dipped his brush into the paint he said, "Well, parts of it were pretty good. They talked about a lot of things, but overall, at least for me, it was a bit of a downer."

I felt myself cringe because the course he attended likely followed a traditional approach to retirement education that is still common today but that, in my opinion, is out of date. It presents a traditional retirement scenario that Dave couldn't relate to.

Retirement lifestyle or non-financial planning has evolved since the 1950s when, motivated by a vague moral concern for employee welfare following retirement, a handful of major corporations developed programs to assist employees through the transition at the end of their careers. Health professionals developed this original approach to retirement education and the subjects covered reflected this orientation. Most programs today continue with this old approach. As a result, some of the issues confuse retirement with ageing, they do not apply to everyone, often include generalizations and subtle moral judgments, and most important of all, can't help Dave with his dilemma.

Based on research I have carried out on retirees plus more than twenty years of conducting retirement education workshops with pre-retirees, I believe the traditional approach is badly in need of revision. That's why I cringed when Dave said the course was a downer.

"What kind of things did they talk about?" I asked.

"Mostly financial," he replied. "Like I said, it was pretty good. Some of the speakers, especially the financial guy, really knew his stuff. But Diane and I have a financial planner who has been advising us for a long time so most of what he presented we already knew."

"Did they go through issues besides money?" I asked.

"That was part of the problem," said Dave. "They talked about retirement being the best time of your life: the "golden years". They don't look too golden to me. Anyway, the guy said we'd have hundreds of extra hours to fill in retirement and he gave examples of what people were doing in retirement like an organization for seniors where they travel and study. But to tell you the truth, I'm not interested in that."

Dave put down his brush and said, "I have the course description. Should I go and get it?"

"Sure, I'm curious to see what they covered."

He returned and I could see the course followed the traditional approach I referred to above. Often these courses include sweeping generalizations about what you should or should not do in retirement. I have seen statements such as; "You should always wait at least a year following retirement before making any changes in where to live," or, "For a happy and healthy retirement you should become involved in something completely different at least once a year", or "Do nothing for at least a year following retirement." Notwithstanding that these generalizations contradict each other, when ever I come across personal opinions and judgments about what people should or should not do in retirement, I react negatively.

"Do you want my opinion of the course?" I asked.

"Why not, you're the expert."

"Looking only at the non-financial side, I have a problem with some of the contents."

"A problem?" he replied.

"What I think, Dave is that you probably have a false impression of what your retirement will or could be like, and I don't think this course helped matters."

"I hope so," he replied. "I keep getting mixed messages about what to expect."

I explained there are two distinct areas of retirement planning: the financial and the non-financial or lifestyle issues. The financial side is based on an established body of knowledge and most financial planners are highly trained accredited professionals. Unfortunately, on the non-financial side anyone can claim to be an expert and the body of knowledge is weak, to say the least. It is not grounded in solid research or theory, is full of value judgments and the standard issues tend to be recycled.

"I refer to this as the traditional model," I said indicating the seminar outline. "It was developed over forty years ago and it no longer applies. Retirees today, people like yourself, are different. Most books and courses, including the one you took, are variations of the traditional model. That's why I have a problem with this course."

Lifestyle retirement education involves many dimensions and issues and given Dave's anxiety, I realized I had to start at the beginning. I suspected that like many people, he really didn't understand retirement. His image was probably out of date and was likely reinforced by the course he took. I pointed out that the first thing he had to do was re-evaluate and update his image of retirement.

"OK," I said. "Let me describe what you can expect. I can assure you that it is quite different from this."

"I don't think that's the problem," he replied. "I have a pretty good idea of what retirement is. My problem is, I'm just not sure if I am ready for it."

Dave's problem ran deeper than he realized. It was not simply a matter of not being sure if he was ready for retirement. His problem stemmed in part from the meaning he attached to retirement, and his subsequent action - or in his case lack of action - toward it.

Definition of the Situation

To appreciate Dave's problem and the solution I present, we can take a brief look at a theory called 'Situational Analysis'[2]. This theory describes how people respond not only to the objective features of a situation, but also, and often mainly,

2. Social scientists base their thinking and research pursuits on established social theory. It provides a framework or vantage point for analysis. My academic interests focused on a group of social psychologists, with a particular affinity for the insights of W.I. Thomas. Writing in the 1920's, Thomas developed a concept called 'the definition of the situation'. For our purposes, he demonstrated that one capacity that differentiates man from animals is that the latter act primarily on instinct, while the former have the ability to examine and deliberate before acting. He referred to to the meaning the situation has for them. This explains why two people faced with the same situation might react to it in totally different ways. If one person sees a glass as half-full, while another sees the same glass as half-empty, we have two different definitions of the same situation (viewing a glass of water). Or if two people attend a movie, one enjoys it, and the other doesn't, again we have different definitions of that situation, and two potentially different ways of reacting to that situation.

Similarly, retirement is a situation that can be defined differently by different people and one would expect to see different meanings of, reactions to, and ways to approach retirement.

Regarding Dave's uncertainty about retirement, I felt he had two problems. The first was that his definition of the situation (his pending retirement) did not reflect reality. It was based on observing the experiences of other retirees, the media, traditional images of retirement, and hearsay. Unfortunately Dave's negative image of retirement was exacerbated by the course he attended. Dave's other problem was that he lacked proper guidelines and tools to help him make the transition from work to retirement.

My plan was to present him with a program I developed called Life Goal Planning, including tools to help ensure his retirement would be worthwhile and enjoyable. Clearly I

---

the act of examination and deliberation as a stage that preceded action. We pause, and consciously or subconsciously try to make sense of a situation, and based on our interpretation or the meaning we attach to that situation (our definition of the situation), we act accordingly. Thomas succinctly presented this insight in a single sentence: "If men define situations as real, they are real in their consequences".

couldn't present the entire course over my fence, but I wanted to present some facts to help him redefine retirement. With a more accurate retirement definition and the tools to aid his transition to retirement, he would be on his way to solving his dilemma.

To underscore the way our definition of a situation impacts on how we react to a situation, I told Dave a joke. "Stop me if you heard it before," I said. "It's about a traveling salesman."

"Go for it," said Dave.

"It's an old joke," I said, "but the message is still applies."

> A salesman was driving home from a very successful sales trip cheerfully thinking about his wife and children who would greet his arrival. All of a sudden, BANG, he had a flat tire. His first impression was, "I'll be late for dinner". But then he thought, "Why worry? So I'll be a little late. I made good money this trip; I'll fix the tire and be on my way". When he opened his trunk he discovered he had no jack. He started to get mad but again he thought, "There's no point in getting upset. I passed a gas station a while ago. It's a beautiful day. I'll walk to the station, get a jack, and be on my way".
>
> After walking a few miles he realized, "I'm in the middle of nowhere, for sure the guy will charge me for the jack. Well, it can't be too much. Anyway, I had a very successful trip, so it doesn't matter". But as he pondered his predicament, he started to worry, "I'm at his mercy - he could charge anything he wants. I don't have any options. He can really

take advantage of me". As he got closer to the station he got increasingly upset expecting to be overcharged for the jack.

When he reached the gas station the attendant approached with a smile and said, "Yes sir, can I help you?" The salesman was so angry, he yelled back, KEEP YOUR !?@}#* JACK! I DON'T WANT IT ANYWAY!"

"Because he expected to be overcharged for the jack," I continued, "he got so angry that he no longer wanted it. Applied to retirement, if a person's image of retirement is negative, if you expect it to be empty and meaningless, you might end up thinking, KEEP YOUR !?@}#* RETIREMENT! I DON'T WANT IT ANYWAY!"

"It's only negative because I'm confused about what I should do," said Dave.

"I realize that," I said. "But to overcome your confusion first you have to clarify your image of retirement."

"If you insist. Start clarifying."

"First," I explained, "I have a confession to make."

He put down his paintbrush, sat on his stool and said, "Start confessing, my son."

I continued to paint and said, "I've been involved in retirement education for more than twenty years, and my confession is that I hate the word retirement."

"You hate it?"

"Not the word itself," I said, "but it has a history of bad press and negative images."

To explain, I asked him to define retirement.

"Well I suppose it means giving up your job; ending your career."

"Yes and no," I replied.

"What do you mean?" he asked.

"Your definition reflects the image most people have of retirement. Even the dictionary defines retirement as withdrawal from active working life. But think about it, Dave. A definition should describe an entity. This definition refers to what you are giving up. It doesn't describe, explain or give us any idea of what retirement is. It's like defining day as not night, or leisure as non-work. And if retirement is defined as giving up work, then we have a problem with people who ease into retirement, or retire and then go back to work. Are they retired, or not?"

"They are semi-retired," he replied.

"My point is, defining retirement as giving up work is the traditional image. It focuses on what people give up, rather than on what they gain. It confuses retirement with health and ageing issues, often including hidden value judgments, and spawning awkward phrases to describe people who have not completely given up work."

"Do you have a better definition?" he asked.

"I think so," I replied. "But first let me ask you another question. Besides giving up work, what other meanings do we apply to the 'R' word?"

"The 'R' word?"

"That's how I refer to the word 'retire' because of all it's negative baggage. But if you looked up retire in the dictionary, what other uses would you find?"

Dave thought for a moment and said, "It means to go to sleep."

"That's a good one. We also use retire to refer to retreat, withdraw or take out of circulation. In baseball, when a batter strikes out, we say the pitcher retired the batter. And we refer to a shy or modest person as retiring. Are you beginning to see the problem?" I asked.

"I never thought about it that way," he replied.

All of these meanings point in one direction - withdrawal. Surely this is not true of retirement today. I can't think of another word in the English language with such a range of images and meanings, most of which are negative. Of course there is nothing wrong with retiring a debt, or going to sleep if you are tired, but when referring to giving up work, business or a career, the "R" word implicitly reflects advanced age and the other negative images. One or two generations ago, retirement saw people leaving work at age 65, the lucky ones with a gold watch and a pension, but most did not lead a particularly fulfilling or lengthy life in retirement, and most did not expect much from retirement. We have only to think of our grandparents, or in some cases our parents, to evoke a picture of retirement that we hope will not apply to us. Fortunately the negative meanings hidden in the "R" word are out of step with the new retirement.

Today we are on the verge of a major upheaval. Eighty-six million Baby Boomers born between 1946 and 1965 are on the threshold of retirement and as a whole, they face a set of life circumstances that are significantly different from those faced by their counterparts in the past. They are richer, will live longer, are more highly educated, expect more from retirement, and account for 56 percent of the adult population. Given these differences, the negativity that accompanies the 'R' word is simply out of step with the new generation of Boomer retirees.

When I conduct group seminars and workshops I use slides to highlight certain crucial points. I stood there with my paintbrush in hand wondering how I could emphasize the next point. Then it struck me. I dipped my paintbrush in the paint can and wrote on the fence.

"This is another use of the 'R' word that really bothers me," I said.

Dave smiled. He knew what I was getting at.

This blatant misuse of the "R" word stretches my tolerance to its limit: Retirement Home. I recall when a Retirement Home was called an Old Folks or a Senior's Home. Clearly we have a problem when homes for the aged are referred to as homes for the retired. A retirement home has absolutely nothing to do with retirement.

"Is it a home for retirees?" I asked. "If so, I don't think either one of us will be ready to retire for a very long time.

"The problem with the 'R' word," I continued, "is that retirement has had its share of bad press and most people don't realize how that can affect their view of retirement. If you think of retirement as giving up work, retreat, withdrawal or going to sleep, clearly you do not have much to look forward to. It can become a self-fulfilling prophecy.

"The good news, Dave, is even if these negative characteristics applied to retirement in the past, there's no reason they need apply to retirement or retirees today."

"Take a look at your friends," I said. "They are future retirees. It should be pretty obvious they won't withdraw when they retire. You can understand why I hate the 'R' Word. It is simply out of step with reality."

"I never thought of it that way," he replied. "But it's true."

I wanted to show Dave how we can re-define retirement to be more compatible with retirement today.

When I started conducting retirement education workshops I recognized the problem with the 'R' word and needed to update the image and definition of retirement. I wanted a new word that would be instantly recognizable, effective, and that would delineate what retirement is, not what it isn't. The word had to be positive and could not make any reference to age because age has nothing to do with retirement. Eventually I came up with my replacement for the 'R' word.

I painted the word "RETIRE" on my fence. Then I said, "We start with the 'R' word and add a dash." I added the dash.

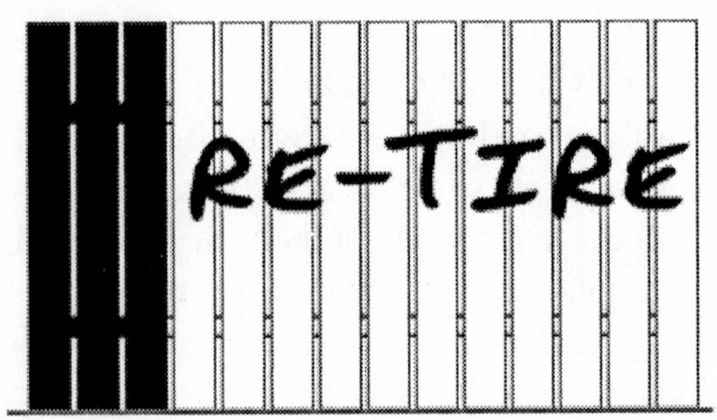

"What image comes to mind now?" I asked.

Dave smiled, "Getting new tires for your car."

"Exactly, the word re-tire with a dash suggests a new set of wheels."

"Actually," said Dave, "I bought new tires a few weeks ago before we went to visit our son."

"And when you got the new tires installed, how did you feel?"

"I felt good. I felt a lot safer."

"Exactly," I replied. "With a new set of wheels you can go anywhere feeling confident the journey will be safe and comfortable. Let it rain. Let it snow. I don't care. I have new tires on my car. Tire manufacturers love this image - it sells tires.

"Now transfer this image to your re-tirement," I explained. "To re-tire with a dash is like getting a new set of wheels for your life. It rejuvenates; you can go anywhere; do anything; please yourself.

"Adding a dash also refers to mixing in something to improve the original like adding a dash of salt or humor. This is precisely what re-tire with a dash involves: spicing up an outdated image of retirement."

This new description characterizes what re-tirees hope to gain from re-tirement. It implies preparation for a journey, movement, action, rejuvenation, freedom, and a fresh new start: a new beginning.

When you re-tire (with a dash), you gain something (a new lease on life). When you retire (without the dash), you give up something (work, your turn at bat). And because re-tirement makes no reference to giving up work, it is possible to re-tire to a new line of work.

A New Frame of Reference

"From now on Dave, whenever you see or think of the 'R' word, spice it up, add the dash. Think of getting a new set of wheels for a new life journey. When the time comes to say, 'I am re-tired', say it with pride."

From this point on, 'Re-tiree' and 're-tired' refer to the rejuvenated individual who is taking the journey, and 're-tirement' refers to the time during which the journey takes place.

"I like it," said Dave.

"Then I think you will like my definition of re-tire."

As I wrote on the fence I said, "Re-tirement with a dash is defined as a career earned from and following work."

"By emphasizing that re-tirement is earned, we acknowledge its worth. It is a reward following work. You have earned something to be proud of."

"Another key characteristic of re-tirement," I explained, "is that it is a career. You may not work in re-tirement, although many people do. However, like your work career, your re-tirement career will develop and evolve over time. The new re-tirement is positive, dynamic, progressive, and makes

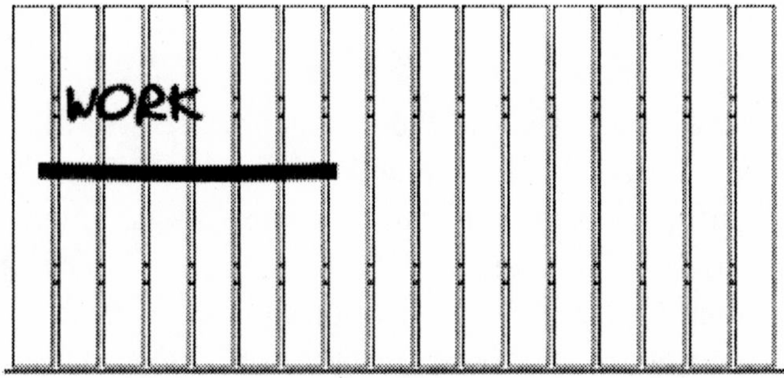

no reference to age. It carries no negative baggage and, because it makes no reference to giving up work, there is no need for awkward phrases like 'semi-retired' when a retirement career includes work."

"Imagine this line represents your work career," I explained. "Most people start their first job and this leads to something else, which leads to something else, and so on. When they reach the end of their work career, often they are doing something completely different from when they started. For most people the direction of their work career is guided not simply by job satisfaction, but mainly by the need for income and security."

Next, I introduced Dave to another career represented by a line parallel to a work career.

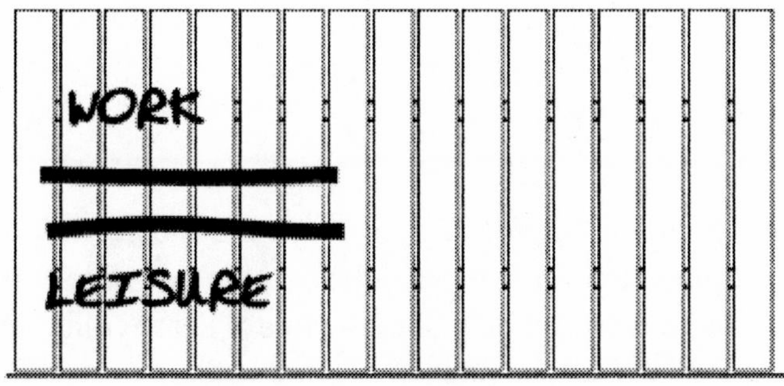

"Leisure can also be viewed as a career. Similar to a work career, it will develop and evolve, but it can also be highly influenced by one's work career. As circumstances change in a work career, parallel changes may occur in a leisure career. This is because we often choose leisure activities to compensate for our work, or other activities as an extension of our work, such as playing golf with a client or friends from work. In some cases there will be no relationship between the two"

Life Career

To complete the image, I included the re-tirement career [illegible] en-
sion [illegible] and
evol [illegible] est
of b [illegible]

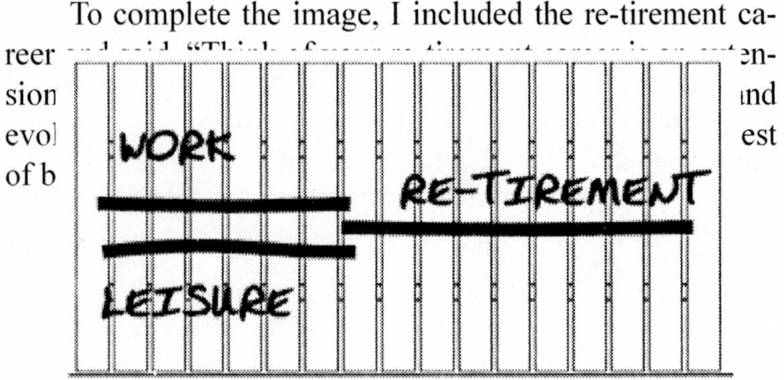

"The main benefit of your re-tirement career, Dave, is that you are the boss. You have the freedom to guide your life so it will be worthwhile and enjoyable. There will be uncertainties but they will be minimized. If you ever feel that something is missing, that you are not enjoying life to the fullest, you have the freedom to make adjustments. Most people do not have this freedom in their working career."

"That's certainly true," said Dave. "But sometimes having all that freedom, or free time, can be overwhelming."

"Absolutely," I replied. "And that is what Life Goal Planning is all about."

"I hope so," he replied. "Because I have nothing in mind now."

"Re-tirement," I continued, "is the opportunity to do something worthwhile and enjoyable. Work responsibilities are behind and you can draw on a wealth of experiences, insights, and aspirations to develop a new career based on the amalgamation of your previous work and leisure careers."

"It all sounds very good," said Dave. "But I still have no idea of what I can do when I re-tire."

"That's understandable," I replied. "I find that about two-thirds of people who attend my Life Goal Planning Workshop do not have any concrete plans for re-tirement. So most people are in the same boat."

Road Map To Re-tirement Happiness

It was clear Dave could use more help than was possible through our backyard chat. I told him that after working with pre-re-tirees for many years, I developed the 'Road Map to Retirement Happiness' for people in his situation. It is a very easy and practical process and would give him the tools to create a worthwhile and enjoyable re-tirement. I suggested we meet again and because re-tirement was a shared experience we should include Diane. He liked the idea, but because

my fence needed more paint we continued to explore concepts to give him greater insight into the new re-tirement; re-tirement with a dash.

"You have to remember, Dave," I continued "There are two forms of spending in re-tirement."

"When most people prepare for re-tirement, they think mainly about financial planning. Of course this is very important, but don't underestimate the significance of how you spend your time on re-tirement happiness."

"But the two are related," said Dave. "It costs money to spend time, you know what I mean."

"I know exactly what you mean," I replied. "I agree they are related. But because there are two forms of spending in re-tirement, there should be two forms of planning for re-tirement. Neither should be left up to chance. Also, because financial planning is based on having a financial goal, which in turn is based on knowing how you will spend your time, the two forms of planning complement each other. That's what the Road Map is all about."

"Now I've met many people who can hardly wait to re-tire because they have a million things they want to do," I added. "But as I mentioned, in my experience almost seventy percent of pre-re-tirees do not have concrete plans."

"I know," said Dave. "That's what frustrates me. I know I have this great opportunity, but I don't want to jump into it quite yet."

To reassure Dave this was very common, I told him about some research on pre-re-tirees. For example, in one study when the subjects were asked how they planned to spend their time in re-tirement, seventy-five percent said 'it's at least somewhat likely they will work for pay after they retire'.[3] This surprisingly large number can be explained by looking at the reasons for wanting to work in re-tirement. When asked why they planned to work, the main reasons for wanting to work included: staying mentally alert (93%), social interaction (86%), and wanting to feel useful (74%). Only 44% said they needed the income.

The message is clear. New re-tirees need to plan how they will spend their time to insure they stay mentally alert, mix with others, and feel useful. Because most people associate these attributes with work, the majority of new re-tirees plan to work in re-tirement. The question is whether or not they will be able to satisfy these needs through work and we shall return to this later.

I told Dave about the research I carried out several years ago when I was teaching at the university. We conducted a major research project among 352 re-tirees.[4] The subjects ranged in age from 52 to 86 years, and had a wide range of occupational experiences, incomes and education. We asked if they were satisfied with re-tirement, and if not, why not. Approximately forty percent expressed some degree of dis-

---

3. Allstate and Matthew Greenwald & Associates, "Retirement Reality Check" Survey, 2004

4. Roadburg, Alan, Aging: Retirement Work & Leisure, Methuen Publications, 1985, p. 95

satisfaction. When asked what they missed most by not being at work, the most frequently mentioned elements included social contact, having something to do, and a daily routine. This result is identical to the reasons given by people who say they want to work when they retire.

I noted that, "Only 9% of the people we interviewed mentioned money as a problem in re-tirement and health was not noted as a major problem either."

He questioned this and said lately he'd read several articles about people in difficulty because they hadn't managed to save enough for re-tirement.

"I'm sure this is true and of course money is important," I replied. "But put in the proper context, it seems that when people re-tire they adapt to their financial situation. Similarly while health obviously influences enjoyment, boredom was the main problem identified by our pre-retirees.

"How you spend your time can be as or more important than money when it comes to re-tirement happiness. This can be good news or bad news. If you don't have a lot of money, it is good to know that you can still enjoy your re-tirement; it is bad news if you are relying solely on money to enjoy your re-tirement."

I asked Dave if he knew of anyone who was well off financially and who was not enjoying re-tirement.

"I sure do," he replied. "You've just described my brother-in-law. He retired a few years ago and was having some real problems. Money-wise he was OK, but he used to be a high-powered executive and my sister complained about him hanging around the house all the time. Eventually he settled down but he went through some rough times. I suppose my friend Les is in this situation, and if something doesn't happen soon, I'm going to be in that situation."

"At the other extreme," I said, "when we carried out our research on re-tirees, we met people living below the poverty line who said re-tirement was the best time of their life. Clearly re-tirement happiness involves more than money.

"The reason my program is called a Road Map," I explained, "is because re-tirement today involves uncharted territory. We need a new guide for re-tirement happiness that focuses on how you will spend your time. And remember, each person's re-tirement is unique. Just because your friend Les is having problems doesn't mean that you will have problems.

"Re-tirement is unique because, unlike other major life changes, there are no dress rehearsals. For example, most people prepare for their first full-time job through school and part-time jobs. This gives them a pretty good idea of what working full time will be like before they start. But re-tirement is different; most people haven't had much experience with extended periods of free time.

"When you were at school you had summer vacation and when you joined the world of work you probably had a few weeks vacation each year. But re-tirement is not like a vacation. Time can be your greatest ally or nemesis. How are you going to use your new freedom? Will it be used to replace the satisfactions lost from work, to help you grow in a way that is satisfying or fulfilling, or will you rely on the vague hope that life will somehow take care of itself? In all likelihood, you could use a little help."

Potential Roadblocks

Before introducing Dave to the Road Map, I wanted to examine potential roadblocks and detours. The first roadblock that can inhibit re-tirement happiness is confusing re-tirement with health and ageing.

"Dave," I said, "As I recall the retirement seminar you and Diane attended included subjects relating to health and ageing. I wonder, what do keeping fit, nutrition and health have to do with re-tirement?"

"Everything, if you're not in good health how can you enjoy your re-tirement?"

"I agree, but would you agree, Dave, that keeping fit, nutrition and good health are important and could affect enjoyment at any stage of life?"

"Of course," he replied. "Health is always important."

"So we agree. Health is important at all stages in life, not just re-tirement, so why should it be part of re-tirement planning? Remember, we are talking about changing from a work to a re-tirement career."

"Because we are getting older and eventually our health may become a problem," said Dave.

"So it's not a health or a re-tirement issue, but an age concern," I replied.

"I guess so," said Dave.

"So we agree that a lecture on health does not belong in a course on re-tirement."

"If you put it that way, I guess not," said Dave.

"The problem," I said, "is if you believe there is a connection between re-tirement and health or old age it could become a self-fulfilling prophecy. You could believe it to the point that you may create a problem. When viewed in the traditional way as withdrawal, putting out of commission, going to sleep, and so on, you can see why some retirement books or courses include a discussion on health. But if you view re-tirement as changing careers, health becomes a separate issue; an important issue, but a separate issue."

I pointed out that re-tirement is not a disease and it never has, nor ever will, kill anyone. If a person is despondent, bored, lonely, or inactive, this can have a negative effect on health and longevity. These conditions, however, are not exclusive to re-tirement. They can occur at any stage in life.

I continued, "As I see it, the only connection between re-tirement, health and exercise is you will no longer be able to use the classic 'I don't have enough time' excuse."

Once Dave realized that ageing and health were not re-tirement issues, we were making significant progress in clarifying his definition of his re-tirement situation.

To continue I explained that it was common to find personal biases and value judgments in books and courses on retirement. For instance, volunteering is often used as the magic panacea for re-tirement happiness. But not everyone wants to volunteer, and to consider volunteering as the 'ideal' re-tirement activity is a personal call that should not be generalized to others.

Glancing at the course outline once again I said, "I see the course included a section on managing stress. Clearly the person who designed this course regards retirement as stressful. If that's the case, I think you would be wise never to re-tire. No wonder you have mixed feelings, Dave."

My favorite example of an irrelevant and inappropriate retirement topic is a discussion on funerals I came across in a book on retirement. It is fairly clear how the author views retirement and the type of negative message this sends to the reader.

Another potential roadblock is the common assumption that re-tirement is similar to leisure. I asked Dave how this issue was presented in his course.

"I remember him saying that retirement was like leisure earned from a lifetime of work," he answered. "He also discussed taking a leisure interest and somehow working it into your re-tirement."

I said, "Actually, Dave, I wanted to talk about this because many people think of re-tirement as similar to leisure. I believe this thinking can hamper the development of your re-tirement career. I agree re-tirement is earned from work, but I do not agree that it is leisure. If you recall our discussion on life careers, I pointed out that your re-tirement career involves a fusion of your work and leisure careers."

To explain this distinction I asked him to define leisure. "I suppose it's doing something unstructured, outside of work. Doing something in your free time," he said.

"That's good," I replied. "And we use the term leisurely to refer to doing something without haste. So, if leisure is defined as free time or doing something slowly, would you say that this is an accurate description of re-tirement?"

"Well it's free time," he replied. "But I hope it won't be too leisurely."

"So we agree. Our definition of leisure does not suit re-tirement. Besides, earlier you agreed that re-tirement was defined as a career earned from and following work."

"Yes," he said.

"Another problem is that sometimes we think of leisure

as secondary or trivial pursuits. But re-tirement is a 'non-trivial pursuit'. Clearly leisure and re-tirement are not one and the same."

Don't just take my word for it. In my research we asked whether or not retirees viewed re-tirement as leisure and in most cases they did not. When asked to define work and leisure, we found an interesting distinction between pre and post-re-tirees. Before people re-tire, they looked upon leisure as free time (similar to Dave's definition). But after they re-tire, because most of their time is free time, they differentiated between work and leisure activities based on degrees of enjoyment. Leisure was defined as enjoyable activities, and work was defined as not-so-enjoyable activities.

This brings us to a common problem for re-tirees who think they can increase the time spent on a former interest, and that it will be as much fun or as meaningful during re-tirement. For example, while we are working, travel generally derives its meaning in contrast to our everyday life and work. The novelty and excitement of travel can wear off, however, if that is all there is to your life. This is not to suggest that leisure interests will not serve the same purpose or will not be enjoyable when one re-tires. Many people have very satisfying lives through spending more time on a former leisure interest. The point is, many leisure interests derive their meaning in contrast to work, and if work is gone the leisure interest can similarly lose its meaning.

Having now warned Dave about potential roadblocks, it was time to give him a few clues about what he could expect in re-tirement.

"What does that mean?" he asked.

I explained it stands for Central Life Focus. This concept originally applied to work, and it implies that work is a dominant sphere in our life. Work exerts considerable influence on your life and demands a significant portion of your time and energy. It influences your thinking, your lifestyle including where you live, your disposable income, your leisure, the friends you choose, and it may even influence whom you choose as a spouse.

"When you stop teaching," I said, "by default re-tirement will become your Central Life Focus. The difference between work and re-tirement as a CLF is that work generally involves a single activity, while re-tirement may be comprised of several activities. Some people need a dominant CLF in retirement while others happily spread their involvement over several activities."

"As we discussed, for some people, a leisure activity can become a Central Life Focus, but for most people since leisure interests derive their meaning in contrast to work, when work is gone the leisure interest is not sufficient to replace a CLF."

"But I have a friend who loves to golf and he could hardly wait to re-tire so he could spend all of his time golfing," said

Dave. "He repairs golf clubs in the winter and is a club marshal. He is totally involved in golf and seems to be quite happy in re-tirement."

"That's a good example," I replied. "And it doesn't contradict my point. He is not just spending more time playing golf - he expanded his interest through other golf related activities. He started a small business repairing clubs and as a marshal is involved in administrative activities. Together these activities constitute his CLF in re-tirement. I bet if he did not expand into other activities and simply played more golf, his re-tirement would not be as fulfilling and he would feel something was missing from his life."

"Here's something else you can expect from re-tirement."

As I wrote on the fence, Dave looked puzzled, "What's that supposed to mean?"

"If you think about it," I said, "re-tirement is like winning a mini lottery. The difference is a lottery pays up front and your re-tirement income will be spread out over your lifetime. Just for fun, suppose you won one million dollars. What would be your main concerns?"

"I wouldn't be concerned about anything," smiled Dave.

"Yes, you would," I said. "First, you would be concerned to make sure your money lasted, and then because you wouldn't necessarily have to work, you would be concerned with what to do with your time."

"But these are good concerns, aren't they?" he said.

"Absolutely," I replied. "And these are the same concerns you must think about in planning for re-tirement. You have to make sure your money lasts, and figure out how you are going to spend your time. Spending time is what the Road Map is all about. By the way, congratulations on your pending windfall."

Diane joined us, saw "lottery' painted on the fence and said, "You guys have been in the sun too long. What's with the lottery?"

I said, "Do you realize how lucky you are to be able to re-tire now you two?"

"What do you mean?" Dave asked.

"Look at your situation," I said. "Why do you think people who re-tire now or who will soon re-tire, are better off compared to retirees in the past?"

"I suppose they'll have more money," Dave answered.

"For sure," I said. "On the average, you are richer than any generation of retirees before you. While you were developing your career, private and public pension plans enabled you to establish an adequate financial base for re-tirement. Also you were aware of the need to save and invest for retirement. That's why you found a financial planner."

"Anything else?" I asked.

"We are healthier and people today will live longer," Diane replied.

"Absolutely, science and medicine have progressed to control or eliminate many diseases, and it has become part of our culture to watch what we eat and to exercise."

The Boomers are also lucky because they are more educated and have a greater sense of personal fulfillment with greater expectations for fulfillment in re-tirement compared to past generations of retirees. Finally, there are more Boomers than any generation of retirees in the past. This gives them political and economic clout.

"So you are lucky to be re-tiring now rather than in the past."

"I guess so," said Dave.

"I have wondered what we could call the Boomers when they re-tire," I said. "When they were younger, they were called Hippies, and then they became Yuppies."

I filled my brush with paint and said, "I suggest we call re-tiring boomers..."

I sat back, admired my work and said, "From Hippies, to Yuppies, to Luckies."

"I do consider myself lucky," said Dave. "But I don't

think it was all luck. We worked hard for our re-tirement."

"I don't mean lucky in that sense," I said. "Don't forget, I defined the new re-tirement as an earned career and implicit in the word 'earned' is the fact that you did not rely entirely on luck.

"Do you remember the old image of retirement (without the dash) that we talked about earlier - retirement as withdrawal from work? Well there was some truth in that image in the past. I believe because of various conditions that did not exist a generation or two ago, you are lucky to be re-tiring now rather than in the past. And that is why I like to refer to re-tiring Boomers as Luckies.

"Besides," I said, "from Hippies, to Yuppies, to Luckies has a nice ring to it."

By this point, it was clear that we had had enough even though my fence was not finished.

"I don't know about you," I said, "but I have had enough for today. I want to continue our talk so why not pick up again next weekend?"

"I'd like that," said Dave. "I'm still waiting to learn about your Road Map."

"I would be happy to share it with you."

"OK," said Dave looking over at Diane. "We can meet at our house next weekend. Would you mind if we called Les and his wife to see if they want to join us? I think he could really use it."

"By all means," I replied. "That's a good idea. In fact the Road Map actually works best with a small group. And since re-tirement is a shared experience it is best if both partners take part. Dave, can you explain to Diane and Les and his wife some of the things we talked about today - like re-tire with a dash and the new way of viewing re-tirement?"

"Sure, and thanks for your help," said Dave. "I'm starting to feel much better about re-tirement."

"You're welcome Dave," I said. "My fence and I both thank you."

As I headed for the house, I looked back at my fence and realized that I got a little carried away. Perhaps Tom Sawyer wouldn't be so proud of me after all.

Chapter Summary

- The traditional approach to retirement lifestyle planning is based on a model developed in the past and is in need of revision.
- The 'R' word – retire - has a history of bad press and negative connotations that do not reflect the nature of the 'new retirement'.
- As an alternative I refer to "re-tire" with a dash. This concept is analogous to getting a new set of wheels to embark on a new life journey.
- Re-tire (with a dash) is defined as a career earned from and following work.
- A re-tirement career will develop and progress guided by your desire to enjoy yourself. It is the fusion of work and

leisure careers. Benefits of a re-tirement career include the freedom to do your own thing and the opportunity to combine something worthwhile with the pleasure of enjoyment.

- There are two forms of spending in re-tirement, time and money. Money alone will not guarantee re-tirement happiness.

- A new Road Map to plan for the non-financial side of retirement is necessary because, a) the traditional model is out of date, b) each person's re-tirement is unique, c) you cannot truly understand what re-tirement will be like until you re-tire.

- Potential roadblocks that can inhibit reaching your re-tirement destination include, confusing re-tirement with health and ageing.

- Re-tirement should not be viewed as leisure. Leisure activities often derive their meaning from work. They can serve to compensate for or be an extension of work. For this reason, a leisure interest may not serve the same function in re-tirement. It may be necessary to develop additional interests in re-tirement.

- Where work as a Central Life Focus involves one activity, in re-tirement it may involve several activities.

- Re-tirement is like winning a lottery. You have a guaranteed income for life and the opportunity to do your own thing

- Re-tiring Boomers are referred to as Luckies because they are lucky to be re-tiring now rather than in the past.

Retired Teachers Research Results

When asked how they felt about the prospect of retiring just before they actually retired, the majority looked forward to it.

Was looking forward to retirement	71.2%
Was neutral about retiring	15.4%
Disliked the idea of retiring	6.9%
Not certain	6.4%

When asked how life in retirement compared to life before retirement, most preferred life in retirement.

Life is better now	62.7%
About the same	31.2%
Life was better before	3.8%
No opinion	2.2%

A similar pattern emerged when asked how satisfied they were with retirement.

Very satisfied	69.6%
Reasonably satisfied	27.8%
Not satisfied	1.3%
Not certain	1.3%

Clearly the majority of retired teachers in our survey looked forward to and were not disappointed by retirement.

(Continued)

"I love not having a schedule. I'm free each day to do what I want to do without arbitrary deadlines. If I don't finish a project today, there's always tomorrow. My husband and I can travel in the fall, winter and spring instead of having to do it all in the summer. I have time once again to read adult books. I have time to spend with my mother (age 89), and I had the time to plan and enjoy my daughter's wedding. My yard and gardens look great and I can work on our farm in the summer, helping with haying and grooming horses."

"I have always enjoyed life! The main attractions of retirement are the openness of the opportunities that are available to everyone. I have always had many hobbies that were not related to work at the school. I had many things that I never had time to do when I was teaching. I have now been able to try out new things. I have traveled and also have worked part time, but at this time I do not think I will work for someone else again. I am having too much fun. Life is good."

"I am glad I am retired. I am particularly happy with the fact, in most instances, I can choose what I want to do each day. I can sleep in, stay up late, go out for breakfast, attend school events or not—as I choose, and can pursue entirely different lines of interest rather than teacher's meetings or workshops. I no longer have to put up with the whims of a principal who was obsessed with being 'in charge'."

2

Do You Want To Know A Secret

(*The Beatles, 1963*)

The following Sunday Les and Janice and I gathered at Dave and Diane's home. Dave had explained to the others what he remembered from our previous conversation.

To begin I turned to Les and said, "I understand that you are re-tired. That's good; we can learn from your experience."

"I don't think I have much to teach anybody," said Les.

"Don't be so sure," I replied. "As I mentioned to Dave last week, you can't truly understand what re-tirement will be like until you experience it. As a re-tiree you are an expert. How long have you been re-tired, Les?"

"About eighteen months now," he replied.

"And what are your impressions so far?"

Les looked at Janice, smiled and said, "I'm not too impressed. It's OK, but at least for me, it's not all that it's cracked up to be."

"What do you mean?" I asked.

"It's hard to explain," said Les. "I'm having a pretty good time but there are times when well, quite frankly, I'm bored. I never thought that would be a problem."

"And you, Janice?" I asked. "Are you re-tired?"

"I worked part-time but I stopped when Les re-tired," replied Janice. "I could go back if I wanted. My housework is a full-time job. And you never re-tire from housework."

"Very true," I replied.

I began to outline my plan. "As I am sure Dave told you, today we will go through what I refer to as the Road Map To Re-tirement Happiness. I covered most of the preliminary stuff with Dave last weekend, so today we'll jump right in. I've been running this workshop for many years and can assure you that it is easy to apply, and if you follow the instructions I can guarantee your re-tirement will be worthwhile and enjoyable."

"That's just what I've been looking for," said Les.

"To start your thinking," I said, "imagine it's a dreary winter day. To brighten things up, you decide to take a holiday in the sun. You visit a travel agent who greets you with a big smile and asks you where you would like to go. You tell him you're not sure, but that you were thinking about Florida. So he pulls out a book of hotel listings, shows you photos of several hotels, and quotes the price including return airfare. Then, after giving you a few minutes to read the descriptions, he asks, "Would you like me to book the holiday?"

"Now let's imagine a different agent. Rather than asking where you would like to go, she asks a few questions about your needs, your likes and dislikes, your interests, your budget, and what you expect from your holiday. After determining these details, she comes up with a different destination, a cruise for example. And let's assume that a cruise had never occurred to you before but turns out to be far superior to the original destination you had in mind.

"The difference between the two travel agents is how they determined your destination. The first agent failed to clarify your destination. He did not provide any service that could not be obtained in a Web site or travel brochure. The second agent took the time to gather a clear understanding of your destination. She realized that your actual destination was not a specific city or location, but the satisfaction of your needs. As a result, she found you a destination more suited to your needs.

"A travel agent's job is relatively easy when it comes to defining the client's destination. Determining your re-tirement destination may take a little work. But it will be worth it because knowing where you are heading, having a clear understanding of your objective or re-tirement destination, is a necessary starting point in your re-tirement career.

"Knowing your destination in re-tirement is crucial," I continued, "because if you don't know where you are heading there is no point in setting out. You can't make any plans or corrections along the way, and how will you know if you get there? Besides, as I explained to Dave last weekend, the way you perceive or look at re-tirement can influence how you approach it. So it is essential that everyone has a clear understanding of their re-tirement destination."

After asking the group where they want to go or what they hope to gain from re-tirement, Les replied, "I guess you could say that I re-tired without knowing where I was heading."

"Join the club," said Dave.

Most people do not have a clear understanding of their objective or destination in re-tirement. When asked this question, the common reply is to identify activities such as travel, spending more time with the grandchildren, starting a small business, spending the winters in a warm climate, golfing, volunteering, expanding on a hobby, and so on. But in fact, activities such as travel, hobbies, volunteering, etc., are only vehicles people use as a means to reach their objective or destination in re-tirement. Activities, regardless of what they are, are not a re-tiree's destination.

Another problem is not everyone enjoys the same activities. We are looking for a destination that applies to all retirees, regardless of age, occupation, gender, marital or financial status.

Because they were having a problem answering this question, I said, "You are overlooking the obvious. I suggest that all re-tirees share the same objective or destination and that is to enjoy yourself. You want a life that is worthwhile, enjoyable, and purposeful."

"That's certainly true," said Janice.

"It's hard to disagree with this," I said. "In fact this objective can apply at all stages of life. The only difference is in re-tirement you have more control over your life and your chance of reaching this objective is greater."

Obviously, concepts such as enjoyment, worthwhile and purpose mean different things to different people. Whether or not something is enjoyable, worthwhile or purposeful depends entirely on the meaning these concepts have for you. The Road Map is based on this assumption.

"Having established that your destination is to enjoy yourself," I said, "the question is, how will you get there? What do you have to do to ensure that your re-tirement will be worthwhile and enjoyable? As Dave and I discussed last week, although important, money alone will not guarantee re-tirement happiness."

"I would agree with that," said Les.

To take this issue to the next level, I asked everyone to write the heading 'Miss from Work' at the top of a sheet of paper.

I recommend that you (the reader) also complete this exercise. Take a sheet of paper and follow these instructions as though you were part of the group at Dave and Diane's house.

"The question to think about is, What will you miss from work when you re-tire? Dave, think about what you would miss from teaching if you gave it up completely. Diane, think about giving up your work and Les and Janice, because you are re-tired, think about what you miss from work. For example, you might miss contact with people or the stimulation. Don't include things that you are quite happy to give up, such as a boss you dislike, office politics, or having to work late. As you write your list I will also come up with a list. Later we will compare our answers."

When everyone completed their list I showed them mine.

I recommend you complete your list of 'things you will miss from work' before turning to my list on the next page.

MISS FROM WORK

Money
Friendships
Routine
Stimulation
Challenge
Satisfaction
Identity
Status
Power

They were surprised when they saw my list. And if you created your own list, you are probably wondering how I knew your answers in advance.

"How does my list compare to yours?" I asked.

"It's practically identical," replied Les.

"Why do you think I was so clever and knew your answers in advance?" I asked.

"I guess you've done this before," said Janice.

"I certainly have. In fact, every time I run my workshop I include this question and as you can imagine, I always get the same answers. Dave and Diane, if you are concerned about giving up anything on your lists when you re-tire, or Les and Janice, if you feel you are missing anything on your lists, you can console yourself knowing it is a common concern.

"Now let's analyze your answers. By thinking about what you would miss when you re-tire, you are in fact listing your reasons for enjoying work. Work is enjoyable because it is a source of money, friendships, routine, challenge, stimulation, and so on.

"But the most important thing you can learn from your list is it identifies your needs satisfied by work.

"You have just made an important shift in your focus from work as an activity, to work as a means for satisfying your needs. By focusing on personal needs, we can explain, for example, why two people could do the identical job, but one enjoys it more than the other. The activity is the same but it satisfies more needs for one person compared to the other. It also explains why work may have been more enjoyable in the past compared to today. The work may be the same today, but its ability to satisfy your needs, say for challenge and stimulation, may have diminished over time. So we have to look at an activity's ability to satisfy our needs, to understand why it is or is not enjoyable.

"Of course a single activity can satisfy more than one need and the more complex the activity the more needs it is likely to satisfy. Work, for example, generally satisfies many more needs than watching television. But even watching TV could satisfy more than one need, such as filling spare time, entertainment, keeping up on current events. And, if you have absolute control over the remote, it can satisfy your need for power!

"Some needs can be met by completely different activities, such as the need for social interaction, while others may only be met by one activity, such as the need for personal mastery of a topic."

The relationship between needs and enjoyment can apply to all activities. For an example, I turned to Dave and said, "Say you and Diane went to an art gallery and Diane enjoyed it more than you did. Can you explain why she enjoyed it more?"

"Easy," said Dave. "Diane appreciates art more than I do so it satisfies more of her needs compared to mine."

We can also interpret these examples from the perspective of Situational Analysis (discussed earlier). As I explained, people respond not only to the objective features of the situation, but also to the meaning that situation has for them. So, if a situation - for example Dave and Diane at the art gallery- is more enjoyable to Diane than to Dave, it is because her definition of the situation (viewing art) includes an appreciation that Dave does not hold.

We had reached the point where I could reveal the secret to re-tirement happiness. I began by summarizing what they had learned so far.

"Your objective or destination in re-tirement," I said, "is to enjoy yourself. The reason we enjoy any activity is because it satisfies our needs. Many of our needs could be satisfied by a different activity at a different life stage. When you re-tire, by default work will no longer satisfy your needs. So, the key or secret to re-tirement happiness is quite simple. All you have to do is find alternative activities to replace satisfactions lost from work.

"That's all there is to it. I told you it was simple, and the beauty is, it works. Remember, your destination or objective is not specific activities. Your destination is to satisfy your needs, especially those lost from work. Re-tirement activities are simply vehicles through which you can satisfy your needs. To apply the road map analogy, your plans are the route you expect to take to reach your destination.

"With the freedom of re-tirement, if you are able to satisfy more needs than those satisfied by work, life will be more enjoyable in re-tirement. On the other hand, if you are not able to satisfy your needs lost from work, life in re-tirement will not be as enjoyable as life before re-tirement. In a nutshell, that is the essence of the Road Map To Re-tirement Happiness."

I waited for this to sink in and said, "What do you think? Does it make sense so far?"

Les was the first to respond. "It makes a lot of sense. I realize now that I was searching frantically for things to do but really didn't know what I was looking for. I didn't think about my needs. I took a music course, but I didn't enjoy it and I'm a lousy musician. Somebody suggested I do volunteer work, but it doesn't really appeal to me. A few of my retired friends are having a great time. It's frustrating."

"It makes sense to me too," said Diane. "At the retirement seminar they talked about how important it was to find things to do in retirement. But they didn't explain it this way."

"Sounds real good in theory," said Diane (the realist). "But how does it work in reality?"

"That's the next step" I replied. "Now that you know the secret to re-tirement happiness and the theory behind the secret, I can show you the process designed to help you find a life after work that you will consider enjoyable and worthwhile."

Chapter Summary

- Your objective or destination in re-tirement is a life that is enjoyable and worthwhile.
- The reason we enjoy or consider any activity worthwhile is because it satisfies our needs.
- In many cases the same need can be satisfied by a different activity at a different life stage.
- When you re-tire by default your needs will no longer be satisfied by work.
- The key to re-tirement happiness (how you will reach your destination) is to find alternative activities that will replace satisfactions lost that used to be satisfied through work.
- If you are able to satisfy more needs than those satisfied by work, life will be more enjoyable in re-tirement. On the other hand, if you are not able to satisfy your needs lost from work, life in re-tirement will not be as enjoyable as life before re-tirement.

Retired Teachers Research Results

The question of what you will miss from work when you retire, was included with the online survey. Your retired colleagues mentioned the following as things they miss from no longer teaching full-time. Note - totals greater than 100% due to multiple responses.

Social interaction	37%
Sense of achievement	23%
Contribution	22%
Involvement	19%
Challenges	17%
Keeping up professionally	14%
Stimulation	14%
Keeping current	12%
Structure/routine	9%
Influence	9%
Responsibility	6%
Nothing	17%

Others missed doing work that really makes a difference, appreciation of the children, feeling productive, a purpose for dressing up every day, and of course several people mentioned missing colleagues and "*interaction with young people who are full of vitality, interest, enthusiasm*"

3

Ticket To Ride

(*The Beatles, 1965*)

At this point I highly encourage the reader to complete the workshop described in this chapter. Read the chapter for an idea of how it works, and then turn to Part 2 for more details. Even if you have retirement plans, you have everything to gain by completing these exercises.

I presented an overview of the full workshop to give Dave, Diane, Les and Janice a general understanding of the process.

"Because everyone is different, the Road Map To Retirement Happiness will not tell you what you should do in re-tirement. What may appeal to me may not appeal to you, and vice versa. It will, however, give you something much more valuable: the tools to ensure your re-tirement will be worthwhile and enjoyable. I have run this workshop with literally thousands of people and I can assure you it works.

"Of course the perfect re-tirement activities may not fall into your lap; it may take time to find them. When I say perfect, I mean activities to replace your needs and skills lost from work. And by referring to activities in the plural, I acknowledge it may take several activities to accomplish this.

You may have to experiment a bit before you find the ones that are perfect for you."

I gave an example I often give in my workshop.

"When you go sailing," I said, "you know your destination – perhaps across the lake, the ocean, or to return to where you started. What you don't know is the route you will take. If the winds are steady and favourable you set the sails and head straight for your destination. If the winds are shifting, which is more often the case, you have to tack, or follow a zigzag course to reach your destination.

"The same process applies to the Road Map. Remember, your destination is not an activity such as travel or playing golf. Activities are vehicles through which you can satisfy your needs. Your destination or objective is to replace satisfactions (needs and skills) lost from work. If conditions are favourable and your re-tirement plans satisfy your needs, you have reached your destination. If not, you will have to make adjustments to reach your destination."

"The Road Map involves several stages. First you will learn how to identify your needs and skills, that is, your re-tirement destination, and how to evaluate activities based on these. Dave and Diane, you can apply this to your re-tirement plans, and Les and Janice, you can apply this to your current re-tirement. Then I will show you how to adjust if necessary and develop new plans."

I have met many people in my workshops who know exactly what they want to do when they re-tire. While that may be so, conditions may change, or what they thought would be worthwhile may turn out not to be. Many people become disenchanted with re-tirement after the initial "honeymoon" phase ends, they get the travel bug out of their system, or find daily golfing is not as fun as they thought it would be. So, whether you have plans for re-tirement or not, it is important to take the time to evaluate what you will do with yourself in the future."

"OK. Let's get started," said Les, anxiously.

"Remember, you are attempting to replace satisfactions lost from work, and this can be a tall order," I said. "You may come up with an inspiration today that serves you well throughout your re-tirement career. More likely you will have to experiment with different activities until you reach your destination. However, I can almost guarantee that if you keep applying the Road Map process, you will reach your destination sooner, rather than later."

Develop Your Needs and Skills List

"Given that your objective or destination in re-tirement is to satisfy your needs and skills lost from work your first task is to find out what these are. By developing a Needs and Skills List you determine exactly what it is you have to replace. You can accomplish this quite simply by answering a few questions about your work and leisure. The complete program includes six questions and the more information you gather the more you have to work with. Today we'll look at two questions. This should give you a good start and you can continue the process later on your own.

"The first question focuses on work. We looked at this earlier and you'll recall the things you might miss turned out to be your needs satisfied by work. So take a piece of paper and on the left side, write the heading 'Needs & Skills'. Dave and Diane, transfer your list of things you will miss when you re-tire, and Les and Janice transfer the things you miss in re-tirement, to your new list. If you wish, add a few new things you hadn't thought of originally. Take a few minutes to do this exercise because these are the main things you may have to replace when you re-tire.

After a few minutes I said, "Satisfactions lost from work refers to both needs and skills. Your list must also include your skills because part of the reason we enjoy an activity is it gives us the opportunity to use our skills. And since skills are transferable, some of your work skills may be used in a completely different context in re-tirement. So think about your skills at work and add them to your list under your needs satisfied by work."

"Sometimes we take our skills for granted because they are second nature. To help think about your skills, imagine you had to find your replacement when you re-tire and ask what skills you would look for in your replacement."

I encouraged Dave to think of skills beyond his classroom skills such as problem solving and communication skills and so on.

I continued, "Of course there is more to life than work and if you want to uncover all your needs, you must also look at leisure. We generally choose leisure activities we enjoy therefore they provide excellent clues to our needs. On the next line of your list, write your leisure activities and then below, list your reasons for enjoying those activities. This is important because it identifies your needs satisfied by those activities. When you finish I will show you how you can put your Needs and Skills List to work."

"Although we haven't answered all the workshop questions (see the remaining questions in Part 2) you have created something valuable," I explained. "Would you agree that if all of the items on your list were met when you re-tired, your re-tirement would be worthwhile and enjoyable?"

In unison, they agreed.

"In that case," I said, "you possess something of value most people do not have when they re-tire. You know your destination in re-tirement: to satisfy the items on your Needs and Skills List. If you satisfy the items on your list your re-tirement will be worthwhile and enjoyable."

Evaluate Re-tirement Plans

The next stage involves evaluating plans. "You now all have a brief list of your needs and skills, and you agreed that if these items were met when you re-tire, your re-tirement will be worthwhile and enjoyable. Now Dave and Diane can use this as a benchmark to evaluate their plans and Les and Janice can use the same process to determine what is missing from re-tirement."

I continued, "Dave and Diane, ask yourselves whether or not each item on your list will be met to your satisfaction given your re-tirement plans. Place a 'Y' next to those needs or skills that you expect will be met, an 'N' next to those that will not, and a question mark next to those that you are not sure of.

"Les and Janice do the same, but because your evaluation will be based on your current experiences there should be no question marks."

I then gave them two examples from my workshop of people who improved their plans as a result of this process.

The first example involved a welder who planned to re-tire to a small farm and set up a welding shop. When he evaluated his plan, he identified 'teaching' as an item on his Needs and Skills List that was not part of his plan. The idea of teaching appealed to him and this prompted him to consider how he could satisfy this need and thereby improve his re-tirement. Although this may seem obvious in retrospect, he did not think about the prospect of teaching welding until he evaluated his plans based on his Needs and Skills List.

I also told them about a couple who planned to move to a high rise condominium on the coast. The husband loved gourmet cooking and the wife had a strong interest in antiques. When they examined their list of needs and skills, they realized that none of these needs were addressed. With a little help from other workshop participants, they came up with the idea of purchasing a small farm in the country enabling him to open a gourmet restaurant and her to sell antiques. This idea opened a new world of opportunities including trips to Europe to purchase antiques and wines.

I asked Dave and Diane if they identified a need or skill that would not be met when they re-tire.

"I found a few," said Diane.

"My problem," said Dave, "is I really don't have any plans, so I don't have much to work with."

"That's OK," I replied. "We'll work on that shortly."

I asked the same question of Les and Janice.

"I can see quite a few things that are missing," said Les. "It gives you a whole new perspective."

How To Create New Plans

"Now it is time to learn how to create new plans (explained in detail in Part 2). As I mentioned, the perfect retirement activities to satisfy your needs will probably not just fall into your lap. You may have to create them and you have to start somewhere; your Needs and Skills List is a perfect starting point. This process works best with a small brainstorming group, such as we have today, but you can also do it on your own. Here is how it works.

"Everyone take some paper and write, 'Suggestions Given' at the top of one sheet, and 'Suggestions Received' at the top of another. The objective of the brainstorming session is to create re-tirement suggestions for each other. When it is your turn, read your entire Needs and Skills List to the group. The others jot down what we think are the reader's key needs and skills. We are then each responsible for coming up with a re-tirement career suggestion for that person. When a suggestion is made, and this is very important, whoever receives the suggestion should write it as given under 'Suggestions Received', and whoever made the suggestion should write it under 'Suggestions Given'."

To start I asked Les, to read his list of needs and skills aloud and for the others to take notes.

When he finished, I said, "Based on Les's needs and skills, can anyone make a suggestion of what he might do to add something new to his life?"

"Les, you used to restore old furniture. Why don't you put an ad in the paper to drum up a small business?" Dave suggested.

I interjected, "OK Les, you have one suggestion. Write it on your sheet headed 'Suggestions Received'. Dave, because you made the suggestion, write it on your sheet headed 'Suggestions Given'."

"OK," said Dave, "but what's the use in me writing down his suggestion?"

"I will explain soon," I replied. "Now, who else has a suggestion for Les?"

Janice said, "Les, you mentioned public speaking as a skill. Why not see if you could teach a course on public speaking?"

Again I reminded Les and Janice to write the suggestion as 'given' or 'received' as appropriate.

Then Diane added, "Les, maybe you could volunteer and help seniors at tax time?"

During the brainstorming exercise I asked everyone to put personal judgments aside to allow ideas to flow. "These are all excellent suggestions," I said. "Les, even if the suggestions don't appeal to you, remember, re-tirement is a career that will evolve; these suggestions can be your starting point."

When everyone had several ideas to work with, I let them in on a little secret that may reveal additional needs and skills for their list and in turn might help them find the perfect retirement.

I said, "Look at your 'Suggestions Given' list. Do you see a pattern in the suggestions you made to others?"

"Actually I see a few things here that appeal to me," said Les.

"Me too," said Diane.

"The reason for this," I explained, "is when you make a suggestion to someone else in essence you are saying, if I had your skill set and interests this is what I would do. So giving suggestions to others is an excellent way to uncover your own additional interests and needs."

"Look closely at the suggestions you gave to others," I continued, "Did you make several suggestions that involved starting a business, teaching, helping others, or joining something? If you see a pattern, or any words that appeal to you, you have identified additional needs or skills to add to your list.

"Now take a look at the suggestions you received. If you identify a suggestion or even part of a suggestion that appeals to you, add it to your Needs and Skills List if not already on your list."

Next we looked at how to tie this all together.

Experience Your Re-tirement Career

"The key to this process," I emphasized, "is to understand that what you end up doing may be the furthest thing from your mind when you originally set out." To reinforce the point, I presented a hypothetical scenario.

"Suppose my re-tirement plans were to spend the winters in a warm climate, to find a part-time job to top up my income, and to take up tennis with my wife. I anticipate that these plans will satisfy my needs. And suppose when I pursue my plan, it doesn't quite work out. I can't find a part time job that interests me. Although we enjoy being away in the winter and playing tennis, I am a bit bored. There is something missing from my life."

"Sounds a bit like me," said Les.

I continued, "To improve my situation I go back to my Needs and Skills List. Suppose I identify friendships as missing so we decide to join a tennis club to take lessons and meet new people. There we meet a couple who invite us to go hiking. We've never hiked before but decide to join them. It turns out we have a great time with their group on the hike. We now spend most weekends hiking and through my revised plans, I am now satisfying more needs including the need for friendships.

"I become heavily involved in the world of hiking. I develop a Web site that includes an active chat room and I start to organize hiking trips to exotic locations. Now we are travelling to scout out potential hiking trips. Lo and behold, I have reached my destination and am satisfying all of my needs. In fact I am satisfying more needs than before I re-tired.

"If somebody had suggested that I become heavily involved in hiking," I continued, "I would have said they were crazy. But because I couldn't find a part time job, was missing friendships and was bored, that led to joining the tennis club, which led to meeting a couple of hikers, and so on.

"So start with an activity. Evaluate it with your Needs and Skills List. If it seems like it will satisfy most of your important needs, go for it; you will never know unless you try. If it doesn't work out, or conditions change, brainstorm some new idea based on your current pursuits, evaluate it, and move on to something better. Continue this process until you reach your final destination that satisfies all of your needs and skills."

"I follow you," said Janice. "But I have a friend, Barbara - she and her husband wanted to travel and spend some time living in a foreign country when they re-tired. Unfortunately her husband took ill and they couldn't travel. What should somebody do then?"

"A very good question," I replied. "Like the song says, you can't always get what you want. Right now what I want is to take a little break. If you don't mind, let's come back to this in a few minutes."

Chapter Summary

- The perfect re-tirement activities will not fall into your lap. You may have to create them.
- The first stage is to identify your Needs and Skills list. Your re-tirement destination is to satisfy the items on this list.
- You can assess your plans based on your Needs and Skills List. This may identify needs or skills that are missing from your plans or current activities.
- To create new plans, brainstorm possible re-tirement career activities based on your Needs and Skills List.
- As your re-tirement career unfolds, what you end up doing may be the furthest thing from your mind when you re-tired.

Retired Teachers Research Results

Now that you have an idea of how the process works, we can look at the types of activities our retired teachers pursue in retirement.

Time with family	52%
Reading	50%
Travel	50%
Volunteering	47%
Exercise/fitness	36%
Gardening	34%
Hobbies	32%
Church related	29%
Work part-time	23%
Home repairs	16%
Caring for parents	13%
Handicrafts	13%
Sports	13%
Substitute teach	10%
Music	10%
Service club	10%
Work full-time	5%

Many re-tired teachers pursue less 'traditional' activities. For example:

Assist with husband's photography business
Genealogy research
Writing/editing newsletter
Elected School Board
Moving to a new home in FL that was hurricane damaged
Water color painting
Working on our farm
Short-term mission trips to Honduras and Mexico
Camping, Hiking, Fishing, Scuba Diving, Prospecting
Built a home
Small business
Continuing education, bridge, book club
Amateur radio operator
Landlording
Educational consultant
Wrote and published my memoirs
Missionary work
8 years full-time volunteering in National Parks
Ballroom dancing and teaching ballroom dancing

"I was immediately sought out to teach at the Faculty of Education; I have done this for six years - ever since I retired. I taught for two years on full contract after having the first two years as a sessional lecturer. I subsequently got elected to the School Board so have dropped back to four courses of Sessional Lecturing in both of the last two years."

(Continued)

"For 2 years I did nothing but exercise every day (Mon - Fri). I became a little 'itchy' and found several opportunities such as refereeing basketball, softball, and field hockey for area school girls' teams. Also, I teach at the local junior college and work part time at the gym where I still work out every weekday. I'm also an officer of high standing and responsibility at two local clubs."

4

You Can't Always Get What You Want

(*Rolling Stones, 1959*)

After a short break, I recalled Diane's question and said, "I agree with you, Diane. It's all very well to talk about finding enjoyable and worthwhile pursuits in re-tirement, but what if for some reason you couldn't do what you wanted to do? Suppose you wanted to find a job but couldn't? Suppose your dreams included sailing but because of medical reasons your spouse has to be on dry land? What if you wanted to travel but couldn't afford it?"

I answered my own question. "You can get what you want, if you find an alternative way to get there. Remember, finding a job, sailing your boat or travel are not your objectives. Your objective is to satisfy your needs. A job, sailing and travel are activities or vehicles through which you can satisfy your needs. The same need or skill can be met through different activities. So if you can't go sailing or find a job, determine which needs you would like to satisfy and find or create an alternative activity that will allow you to satisfy most if not all of those needs."

I told them about a couple from a workshop who wanted to move to the coast and spend time sailing their boat when they re-tired. That situation was similar to her friend Barbara's situation. Unfortunately, just before they were about to move, the wife took ill and her doctor advised against this plan. They were devastated. What could they do? They had been planning this move for a long time.

Basically, they had two options. They could abandon their plans and do nothing, or, they could look for an alternative. Realising that their plans were to satisfy certain needs and skills, they sat down and identified those needs and skills. Then, given the wife's medical needs, they brainstormed an alternative and ended up buying a trailer and travelling the coast. Although their alternative was not quite as ideal as sailing, it was nevertheless another way they could satisfy most of their travel needs, including the additional need of immediate access to health care, if necessary.

This is an important point, so I followed up with another example.

"Remember I mentioned a welder who improved his retirement plans when he identified teaching as one of his needs? Suppose after he moved to the farm he approached the local school to teach welding. And suppose the school didn't need a welding teacher. What do you suggest he should do?" I asked.

"He could look for another job," said Les.

"That's true," I replied. "But suppose his needs were focused more on teaching than on earning money. It wasn't a job he was after. He simply wanted to pass his skill on to someone else."

"Maybe he could teach somebody on his own," suggested Diane. "You said that he was going to open his own workshop. That would be perfect."

"Good suggestion Diane," I said. "His main concern was to satisfy his need to teach. If he can't do it through the school, he may be able to find an interested kid who would love to learn how to weld and he could teach him or her on his own. Or, maybe teach something else altogether. If his need to teach welding in a school was great enough, he may decide to go back to school and become a teacher. Who knows? Remember, re-tirement is a career that will develop and evolve and sometimes you never know where you will end up."

Ace Up Your Sleeve

"The point is," I emphasised, "You have an ace up your sleeve. If there is something you want to do but for some reason you can't do it, you have the tools to find or create an alternative. You do not necessarily have to rely on others as you progress through your re-tirement career. This is in stark contrast to the work career experienced by most people.

"Say somebody wanted to find a job, or had a job and hated it. The same needs may be satisfied through self-employment or a nonpaying activity. If you can't afford to travel, you can organize a group and maybe have your way paid by a travel agency, or travel on a freighter, or find something completely different - as long as it satisfies your needs. If for some reason you are prevented from pursuing anything, the process I described earlier will allow you to create a worthwhile and enjoyable alternative. Who knows, your alternative may be a blessing in disguise. It may turn out to be better than the original.

Looking for a job is similar to looking for any activity in re-tirement, the only difference is a job satisfies (in varying degrees) an extra need, money. For example, if you couldn't find a job, you might start out cutting other people's lawns. Not a very stimulating activity, but you have to start somewhere. One day a customer asks you if you paint driveways. "Of course," you reply. "For an extra $75 I would be pleased to paint your driveway." So now you are a gardener and a driveway painter. Realising that there may be a need for driveway painters; you place a small ad in the local paper advertising your services. Happily, the response is significant, so you hire another re-tiree to help you. Eventually you end up with eight employees doing the work for you. As an added bonus, you are free to travel in the winter - supported, I might add, by your additional summer income.

Although this example is hypothetical, you can see the underlying theme. Start doing something, apply the techniques briefly outlined here and in more detail in the Appendix, and eventually you will find the perfect activity that will satisfy your needs and skills.

There is the possibility of rejection even in a non-work situation. I told them about Richard who sold his business and in thinking about what he could do in re-tirement, discovered a government agency that paired re-tired business people with young entrepreneurs. He had developed a very successful business and was quite excited about the prospect of sharing his 'street smarts'. By the way, he had never volunteered before. He contacted the agency and was told that they had too many re-tired business people and not enough interested entrepreneurs. Although this was not a personal rejection, in essence he was told that he wasn't needed. Richard felt rejected and deflated.

But, and this is hypothetical, Richard learned something. He learned that the agency did not have enough entrepreneurs signed up. This could open up a new avenue for him.

Perhaps he could approach the agency and volunteer to find entrepreneurs; he still had many business contacts from the past. Or he could talk to others who felt like him and together they may be able to develop some alternative method to help others. Once the creative juices begin to flow, opportunities are endless.

"Remember," I said, "your destination or objective is to satisfy your needs. If for some reason you can't participate in one activity, simply find an alternative activity to satisfy those needs. This simple fact is at the heart of a successful re-tirement career."

As a winner of the re-tirement lottery you have the time, and now you have the Road Map and tools to create a future that is worthwhile and enjoyable. All you have to do is put them to work.

I knew that Dave was still troubled by the question of whether or not to join his son-in-law's business, so I turned to that issue next.

Chapter Summary

- If you know what you want to do in re-tirement but for some reason cannot do it, determine which needs you would like to satisfy and find or create an alternative activity that will allow you to satisfy most if not all of those needs.

- You have an ace up your sleeve. You have the tools to create alternative activities if you can't get what you want.

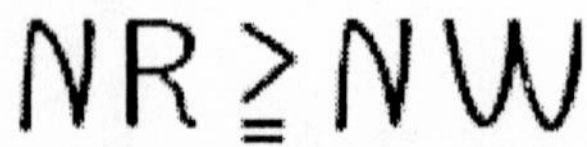

5

A Hard Day's Night

(*The Beatles, 1964*)

Working in re-tirement is not for everyone. However it is not uncommon for people to think about this prospect. Earlier I referred to a study where seventy-five percent of the subjects said that it was 'at least somewhat likely they will work for pay after they retire'.

Turning to retirees who are working in re-tirement, one study surveyed a sample of older workers (ages 50-75) looking into the reasons for working in retirement [5]. They found that 89% said they did so *'to keep active'*. Other common responses included: *'had free time'* (73%), *'to maintain social contacts'* (68%), *'desire for additional income'* (63%), *'not ready to retire'* (58%), and/or *'to maintain their profession and professional contacts'* (56%). Only about two in five (41%) said the reason was a *'need for additional income'*.

If you plan to earn money in re-tirement full or part-time, the Road Map to Re-tirement Happiness can help you

5. Moen, Phyllis, et al., 2000, The Cornell Retirement and Well-Being Study: Final Report, Ithaca, New York: Bronfenbrenner Life Course Center, Cornell University.

decide if this is your best course of action, and if you have several different opportunities, it can help you choose the best option – the one that will satisfy more of your needs.

To start the discussion, I turned to Dave and said, "Dave, I recall a while ago that you said you might consider going back to work when you re-tire. Is that true?"

"Yes," he replied. "It's funny. The idea of re-tiring has some appeal, but I don't want to quit working. I have a few ideas including joining my son-in-law with his business. I would like to find something interesting, maybe just part-time."

Taking The Easy Way Out

"First of all, Dave," I said, "like most re-tirement issues, I can't tell you what to do. For some people working in re-tirement is the best course of action, and it can be the opposite for others.

"Having said that, I highly recommend that as part of the decision process you ask yourself a very important question. And you should try to be honest with your answer. The question is, in your desire to replace satisfactions lost from work, are you taking the easy way out by going back to work?"

"What do you mean?" he responded.

"Well, have you given serious thought to why you are thinking about going back to work when you re-tire?"

"Sure I have," he replied. "I enjoy my work and I may have to keep earning when I re-tire. But it's mainly because I enjoy my work. I think I would be lost with nothing to do. Besides, Diane doesn't want me hanging around the house. I have to find something to do when I re-tire."

"That sounds like good reasoning," I said.

I asked the others if they could think of other benefits to working in re-tirement.

"It gives you the opportunity to be with other people and it can be stimulating," suggested Diane.

"Absolutely," I replied. "We talked about this earlier. Besides money, work can satisfy many needs including friendships, routine, getting out of the house, challenge, stimulation, identity, and so on. Some people work in re-tirement because they need the money. Others go back to work to satisfy these additional needs. There is nothing wrong with this providing you consider it to be worthwhile and enjoyable - providing it satisfies your other needs. If it didn't turn out this way, I take back my endorsement."

Obviously, if a person had to earn extra money it may be necessary to ignore the non-monetary needs in order to satisfy the need for extra income. I encouraged Dave not to rush into anything - to pause and take stock of his situation. I didn't have to remind him that besides its positive benefits, working could hold some potentially negative consequences.

"I realize that," said Dave. "And that's why I am having a problem deciding. Eric, my son-in-law is encouraging me to join him."

"The problem is," I continued, "working in re-tirement is not necessarily a magic panacea. It can have a down side. Although it may satisfy some of your needs, including earning money, working in re-tirement can impose restrictions and it may not satisfy all of your important needs. And as we all know, the key to re-tirement happiness is to satisfy your important needs."

Evaluating Work

To help evaluate whether or not working was Dave's best solution, I told him to take a look at his Needs and Skills List and to identify the five most important needs or skills that must be satisfied when he re-tired. I asked him to think about each item, to be honest and to list these items on a separate piece of paper.

When he completed his list I asked, "Did you include money on your list?"

"Yes," he answered.

Then I said, "If you had to identify two items in your top five list that must be part of your re-tirement, would earning money be one of them?"

"Probably not," he replied.

"In that case," I asked, "would you agree that money is not your main motivation for working in re-tirement?"

"I don't know," said Dave. "Right now things look OK, but you never know what will happen in the future. The stock market is unpredictable so of course the financial side is very important."

"I am not denying that," I replied, "but there are many more things to consider when making the decision to re-tire or whether or not to work in re-tirement."

To help him think about this decision more clearly, I suggested that he imagine or think about working for his son-in-law and ask himself whether or not the items on his Needs and Skills List, especially his top 5 needs, would be met. I acknowledged that this may be difficult now and that he may have to wait until he started working for his son-in-law.

I suggested that he could add additional needs that did not appear on his original Needs and Skills list. These could include things like sleeping in, spending time with Diane, not being tied down, and so on. This exercise would also give him a better idea of what type of activity to look for. For example, if stimulation or spending more time with Diane were high on his list of priorities, he should bear this in mind when deciding about working in re-tirement.

Because Dave was thinking about going into his son-in-law's business, I said, "Of course I don't have to remind you Dave that working with family members can present additional problems."

"I realize that," he said.

"To my mind," I replied, "the most important thing to look out for is to make sure that if your business arrangement doesn't work out, that it doesn't affect relations within the family. So I highly recommend that before you make any move you discuss this aspect fully with your son-in-law."

"I will," he replied. "We have a pretty good relationship and he's a good guy. But I understand what you are saying."

"If you start to work for Eric," I continued, "and if things are not going well, don't forget that you have an ace up your sleeve. Consider this as one step in your re-tirement career. You have the tools to get you to the next step. Who knows, you may discover an idea that may never have occurred to you had you not started to work with Eric. So even if it doesn't work out, you may be able to benefit from it."

I warned Dave about the possible consequences if the job did not work out. This could apply to anyone looking for work in re-tirement. That is, suppose you apply for a job and are turned down. You may not be too concerned if it happened once. But if you apply for several jobs and still turn up empty, this can affect your sense of self-worth or esteem.

Before you re-tire, you probably had a relatively strong sense of self-worth and feel valued as an employee. But if you are rejected by a number of potential employers, you may begin to feel down. I am not suggesting that you will not find a job. I have no way of knowing your value in the work force. But if you experience a number of rejections, don't take this to heart - it is a fact of life that does not necessarily reflect on you personally.

Finding a job can be difficult for anyone at any age or stage in life, not just at re-tirement. But remember, you have an ace up your sleeve. You do not have to abandon your thoughts about work or earning money. All you have to do is apply the Road Map techniques to create or develop an alternative way to satisfy your needs, which may or may not include earning money.

"When you complete this exercise, Dave, you may have additional insight into whether or not working in re-tirement is for you. On the other hand, if you are playing with several different options, here is what you can do. Choose plan A and evaluate, as we did earlier, which needs and skills it will satisfy. Then, create a new column for Plan B, next to Plan A, and go through the same process of evaluating that plan. It's possible that you will discover which plan is preferable – that is, the one that will satisfy more of your needs and skills.

"At any rate," I continued, "if you work part-time you will still be looking for other activities to fill your remaining free time. Remember, your objective is to satisfy your needs and it may take more than one activity in re-tirement to replace all needs satisfied by work. So, if you work part-time, identify those needs that are being met and those that are not, and focus on the latter for your non-work interests in retirement. Eventually you may want to or will have to re-tire completely, so bear this in mind when looking for, or creating new non-work interests.

"If you start to work and if things are not going well, don't forget that you have an ace up your sleeve. Consider this as one step in your re-tirement career. You have the tools to get you to the next step. Who knows, you may discover an idea that may never have occurred to you had you not started to work part-time in the first place. So even if it doesn't work out, you may be able to benefit from it."

Chapter Summary

- If you are thinking about working in re-tirement, ask yourself if you are taking the easy way out to replace satisfactions lost from work.

- If so, there is nothing wrong with this providing you are still able to satisfy your main non-monetary needs.

- Working after re-tirement can have a down side if you have to sacrifice satisfying some important needs in order to earn money and if earning extra money is not your top priority.

- The exercise outlined in this chapter can help you decide: a) if you want to work in re-tirement, and b) if so, which type of work is best for you.

Retired Teachers Research

Expect to work for salary after retirement

Yes	27%
No	57%
Not certain	16%

Have worked for salary since retiring

Yes	62%
No	38%

It is interesting to note that only 27% of teachers expected to work before they retired; yet after retirement 62% were involved in some kind of remunerative activities. In contrast, among the subjects in a study mentioned earlier, 75% expected to work in retirement.

Teachers who worked in retirement, 86% worked part-time, and 55% involved teaching. Those who worked at non-teaching activities took part in a wide range of work setting. For example:

Administrative
Agriculture
American Cancer Society
Assessment testing (Nation's Report Card)
Bus tour guide for the lifestyles of the rich and famous in the Hamptons
Church organist
Civil War Sutlery for reenactments
Clerical - Vocational coordinator

(Continued)

Consulting
Coordinated formation of community collaborative
Cruise line
Custodial (low stress) work
Customer service (mall)
Designing and sewing costumes
Directing musicals and plays
Driver education instructor
Drove school buses
Executive assistant to the Leader of a Provincial Party
Funeral home hostess
Golf course
Government elected official
Group facilitation and corporate training
Insurance Sales
Marking ESL papers
Mayor
Politics
Praxis III Assessing
Radio Talk Show
Receptionist
Retail, restaurant
Sales
Self-employed
Taxi driver
Teaching knitting and sewing
Trained M.D.'s in molecular medicine in human cancer
Travel consultant
Truck driving
U.S. Investigator
University 'standardized' patient for Medical staff
Seasonal tax professional, bank director

Reasons For Working In Re-tirement

Teachers who worked in retirement were asked if their main reasons for working were mainly financial or non-financial

Financial only - wanted extra money	8%
Non-Financial - wanted to do something	33%
Combination of financial and non-financial	59%

Clearly, retired teachers chose to work for reasons beyond money. When asked for their non-financial reasons for working in retirement, they replied:

Mixing with people	65%
Satisfaction	62%
Stimulation	55%
Challenge	50%
Having something to do	40%
Contribution	32%
Purpose	28%
Routine	16%
Recognition	8%
Power	5%

Other Reasons For Working in Re-tirement

Creativity and contributing to life.
My own personal recognition of what I could accomplish outside a classroom
Enjoy the teenagers
Keeping up with educational trends
Having an opportunity to visit schools again, teachers/principals, etc...
The challenge of serving in other positions in other school districts
Helped a friend out
Worked for cruise line to earn discounts on cruises
Helping children
To help a fellow teacher
Continuing use of my expertise
Share my experience

"I really enjoy 'teaching ' again. I don't have to deal with unruly students or parents at the college. My other positions are because I enjoy keeping busy and mixing with people."

"Still enjoyed being around children but not having the paperwork. Loved being a substitute a few days a week."

(Continued)

Volunteering

Involved with unpaid voluntary or charitable activities in retirement

Yes	85%
No	15%

Involved with voluntary activities before retirement

Yes	67%
No	33%

Although a high percentage of teachers took part in volunteer activities after they retired (85%), a significant number (67%) had taken part in voluntary activities before they retired. This suggests that only about 18% took up volunteering as a new activity in retirement.

6

(Money) Can't Buy Me Love

(*The Beatles, 1964*)

So far I had treated Life Goal Planning as though it was an entity separate from financial planning. In fact, Life Goal Planning can be an integral part of financial planning and it was important for the group to understand this connection.

I am not a financial planner; my experience lies with the non-financial side of re-tirement education. Having said that, I have worked closely with many different financial planners and advisors over the years conducting Re-tirement Education workshops. And it appears to me that financial planning on its own is not re-tirement planning; it is money management planning. I would argue that Life Goal Planning is the missing element that can transform financial planning into re-tirement planning. Because people spend both time and money in re-tirement, true re-tirement planning requires both Life Goal and financial planning.

To explain this to the group, I said, "Let's change the focus a little bit and look at the connection between Life Goal and financial planning."

"But I'm already re-tired," said Les. "It's too late."

"I realize that," I acknowledged. "But the benefits of combining the two can apply anytime before or after re-tirement and they can apply to areas that may surprise you."

"But Dave and I have a financial planner," Diane added. "And he's done a good job in spite of the ups and downs of the market."

"That's great," I said. "But tell me, when you first started with him how did he set up your plan? What I mean is, did he sit down with you to determine a financial goal for re-tirement?"

Dave looked at Diane with a quizzical look on his face and replied, "Yes I think he did."

"Don't you remember," said Diane. "We spent a lot of time with him in the beginning and he asked us a bunch of questions to get an idea of our financial situation."

"How did you establish your financial goal?" I asked.

"I don't remember," said Dave.

Establishing a financial goal is central to developing a financial plan – you have to know where you are heading before you can devise a plan to get there. The problem is most people don't have all the information they need to es-tablish a financial goal. As I mentioned to Dave earlier, close to seventy percent of pre-re-tirees I meet in my workshops do not have concrete plans for retirement. So they or their financial planners have to take an educated guess to identify a financial goal.

Also, some people may not need that much in re-tirement, while others may need more. For example, if Dave worked in re-tirement he may not need as much as he originally planned for. To compound the problem, financial conditions could change significantly at any time before or after re-tirement and the financial plan should account for these differences. This is where Life Goal Planning comes in.

"Most people think that financial planning is re-tirement planning," I said. "In a sense it is of course, but let's not forget that in order to plan for something, you have to have a pretty clear idea of what you are planning for. Earlier we talked about the similarity between planning a vacation and retirement in terms of making sure you reach your destination. To take this analogy one step further, when you plan a vacation you don't start by asking how much it will cost. First you have to determine..." I listed them on a piece of paper

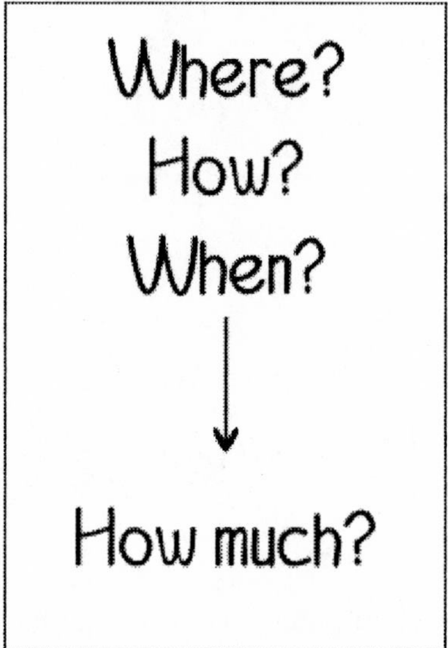

"You have to decide where you are going, how you will get there and when you will leave. Then you can figure out how much the vacation will cost. After estimating the cost, if you decide that it costs too much and you still want a vacation, you can adjust some of the other variables. For example, you can find a less expensive location or travel during low season."

The vacation analogy was straightforward. To apply it to financial planning for re-tirement, I added a few notations to the vacation sheet and explained the items that I had checked off.

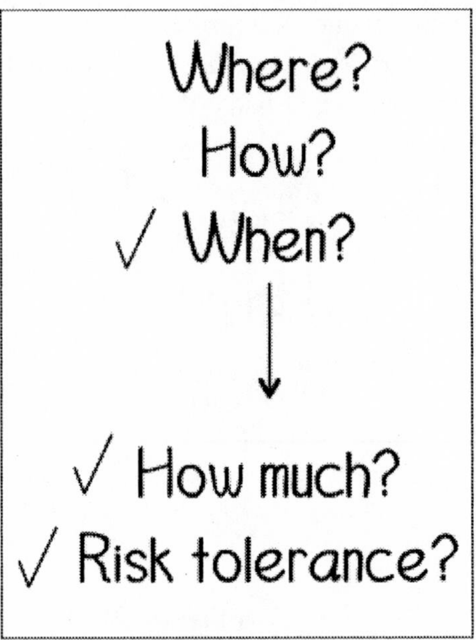

"Most financial plans," I said, "include the same variables as planning a vacation, plus an investment risk tolerance level. The most important element in a financial plan is to have a financial goal - that's the 'how much' factor on our sheet. If you don't have a goal, how can you create a plan? So before you can set up a financial plan you should have an idea of how much money you will need in re-tirement. That's your financial goal.

"The Re-tirement Road Map," I explained, "can supply the crucial missing ingredients that will enable you to truly personalize your financial plan. First, you know your destination in re-tirement (Where?). We spent some time on this. Your objective or destination is to satisfy your needs and skills, especially those lost from work. You know how to identify these items, so you should be able to identify your destination with some degree of accuracy. Second, your route (How?) includes the plans you have made to reach your destination. You have learned how to evaluate and perhaps improve on a plan, and how to come up with new plans. If you include when you plan to retire and your risk level, you have the core information you need to develop a sound basis for estimating your future financial needs or goal (How much?).

"Another way to look at this connection is both Life Goal and financial planning share the same objective. They both involve helping you plan for a life after work that will be worthwhile and enjoyable. The difference is financial planning focuses on how to finance or fund a future lifestyle, while Life Goal Planning focuses on how to find a future lifestyle – but not just any lifestyle, one that will enable you to replace satisfactions lost from work. The connection is in the two key words 'finance' and 'find'. Planning how to get there, and making corrections along the way, starts by knowing where you are heading.

"Let's look at a different scenario," I said. "Suppose you re-tire or are re-tired and your financial situation changes and you find you have a financial shortfall."

Les seemed to perk up at this point, so I explained, "Suppose you determine where, how, and when you are going to re-tire and you discover that your financial situation will not support your intended re-tirement lifestyle. You have an imbalance with a financial shortfall. You know how you would like to spend your time in re-tirement but your financial situation won't support your plans." I drew this scenario on a piece of paper.

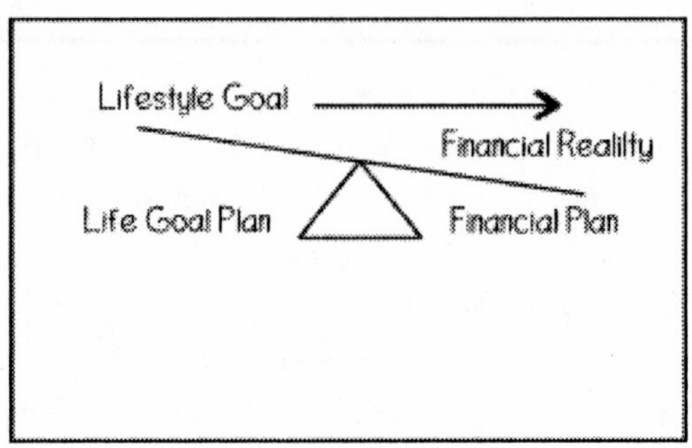

"In this diagram," I explained, "your financial reality at re-tirement is not in sync with your lifestyle plans. You know what you want to do but realize that you have a financial shortfall. To increase your re-tirement income you can make certain adjustments on the financial side. You can work longer, invest for a higher return, or sell assets. In other words, you can adjust the financial side of this teeter-totter to make it balance with the lifestyle side."

"But suppose you don't want to or can't adjust the right side of the teeter-totter. Suppose you can't stay at work longer, or you don't what to increase your investment risk, or sell assets. If you look strictly for a financial solution you may be in trouble. Well, there is a solution. You can adjust the left side of the balance. Remember, the secret to re-tirement happiness is to satisfy your needs, and the same need or skill can often be satisfied by a different activity. Therefore, to make the teeter-totter balance, all you have to do is find alternative activities that satisfy your needs and at the same time are more attuned to your financial reality at re-tirement. Something like this." I redrew the diagram.

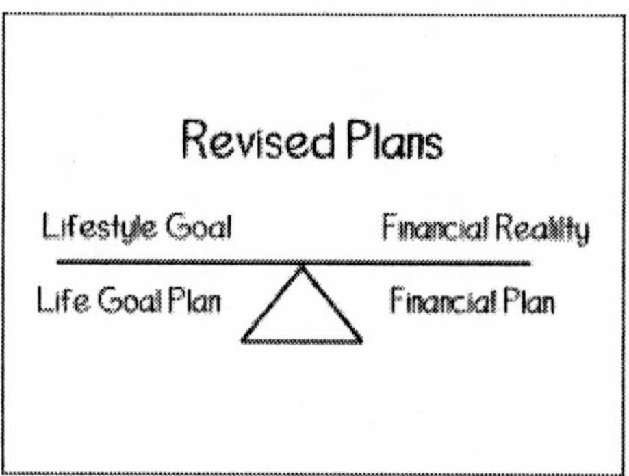

As they looked on I said, "You can work backwards, like we did with the vacation plans. If you can't afford your original re-tirement plans, you can adjust the lifestyle variable to replace satisfactions lost from work by creating alternative activities. Who knows, you may end up doing something better than your original plans.

"The main point is, like I said earlier, Life Goal Planning is your ace in the hole. You have the tools to adjust the lifestyle dimension and you do not have to rely totally on the financial dimension for your re-tirement happiness. Presumably if you were in this situation you would make adjustments to both sides of the teeter-totter. It gives you another option."

I was not finished with this discussion. I still wanted to talk about the decision to re-tire (When?) because this was the issue that Dave originally presented when we were painting my fence. After all, he spent an entire afternoon painting my fence and I still hadn't looked at his dilemma.

I acknowledged that the decision when to re-tire was no longer relevant to Les and Janice, and said, “Dave, it’s time to take a look at what we talked about when we first started this discussion. You mentioned that you were thinking about re-tiring but were not sure when.”

“That pretty well sums it up,” he replied.

“Let’s take a look at how Life Goal Planning can help you with this decision,” I said.

“Finally!” replied Dave. He addressed the others and said, “I painted this guy’s entire fence and somehow he avoided this question.”

“I wasn’t avoiding it Dave, it’s just that I had a few things to explain first so you would truly appreciate how the Road Map can help you with this decision.”

“I know,” he replied. “I was only kidding. I actually have an idea of what I can do. But, go ahead, spell it out for me.”

“Here’s how it works. Start by taking a hard look at your financial situation, and then apply this simple formula.”

I reached for another piece of paper.

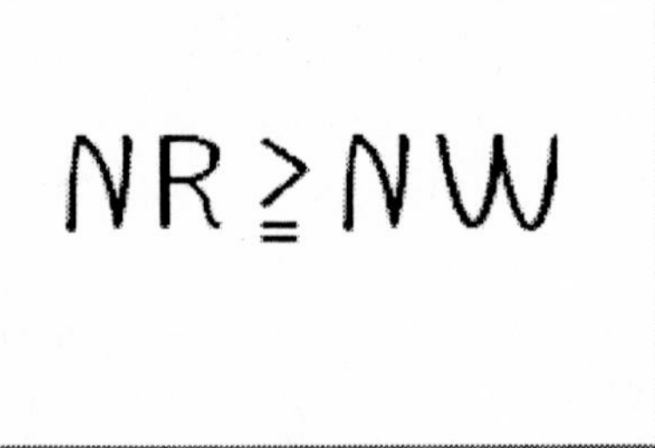

"I have never come across that formula before," said Dave. "What does it stand for?"

"It's a shorthand formula," I said. "NR stands for needs in re-tirement, and NW stands for needs at work. So it reads, you should consider re-tiring when your needs met in re-tirement will be greater than or equal to those currently met at work."

Dave studied my formula and said, "Sounds a bit formal, but that's an interesting way to look at it. How can I figure this out?"

"It's very simple and you're halfway there," I replied. "Remember earlier when you evaluated your re-tirement plans to see if they would meet your needs and skills? Although we only included a few questions, you should have a pretty good idea of those needs and skills that will be met when you re-tire. That takes care of the left side of this equation.

"For the right side, to see which needs and skills are met through your work, you can create another column next to the column where you evaluated your re-tirement plans. In this case ask yourself whether or not each item on your Needs and Skills List is being met to your satisfaction through your work and leisure right now. You can go through each item and place a 'Y' next to those needs or skills that are being met, and an 'N' next to those that are not being met. Because you are evaluating your current life there are no question marks; the answer should be either yes, or no. After you assess your life now, compare it to the life in re-tirement column to see which sphere will satisfy more of your needs and skills. Obviously your decision to re-tire will involve more than this simple exercise, but it can be very revealing and an eye opener when you complete it."

It was getting late and it was time to wrap things up, so I told them I had covered the issues that I wanted to present and that hopefully I gave them an idea of how the process works. I encouraged them to redo the exercises on their own or with a group.

"We definitely will go through it again," said Les.

"So will we," said Dave.

"Glad to hear it," I said.

I thanked them for being such an attentive group and got up to leave. They thanked me and once again assured me that they would complete the exercises as soon as possible.

As I got up to leave, Diane asked if my wife and I were going to attend the block party. I told her we were planning to attend and that we would see her and Dave at the party. As I left they were discussing inviting another couple to join them in a few days to go through the workshop in more detail.

Chapter Summary

- Both Life Goal and financial planning for re-tirement have the same objective – helping to plan for a life after work that will be worthwhile and enjoyable

- The difference is financial planning focuses on how to finance a life after work, while Life Goal Planning focuses on how to find a future lifestyle that will be worthwhile and enjoyable. Planning how to get there, in other words, and making corrections along the way, starts by knowing where you are heading.

- Life Goal Planning is the missing ingredient that turns financial planning into re-tirement planning.
- By focusing on how to find a life after work that will be worthwhile and enjoyable, Life Goal Planning can be instrumental in identifying a financial goal, hence can be integral to personalizing a financial plan.
- Life Goal Planning can provide an alternative if there is a financial shortfall at re-tirement, as well as valuable insights into the decision to re-tire.

Retired Teachers Research Results

Seventy-two percent of the teachers in our sample received some form of pre-retirement planning assistance before they retired.

Pre-retirement planning provided by:

Teacher's Federation	49%
State/Provincial Teachers Retirement System	36%
Financial planner	17%
Employer	5%

Others mentioned learning from former teachers or reading the literature.

The content of the planning assistance included:

Mostly financial	73%
Half financial, half lifestyle	26%
Mostly lifestyle (non-financial)	1%

(Continued)

Areas of Retirement Planning

Although fourty-two percent indicated that they were fully prepared for retirement, areas of retirement planning they wish they had given more attention to included:

Financial planning	27%
Should start earlier	27%
Both financial and lifestyle planning	20%
Lifestyle (non-financial) Planning	14%
Not certain	12%

Level of Satisfaction with Preparations for Retirement

Very satisfied	42%
Reasonably satisfied	51%
Not satisfied	5%
Not certain	2%

Lesson Learned

Most retired teachers took part in a formal retirement education program put on by a Teachers' Federation or a state or provincial retirement system. The primary emphasis was on financial issues. Although over 90% were very or reasonably satisfied with the level of preparation for retirement, the main lessons to be learned are a) Start the planning process early, and b) Include non-financial or lifestyle issues within the planning process.

7

Did You Ever Have To Make Up Your Mind

(*Lovin' Spoonful, 1965*)

Every summer our neighborhood gathers for an informal block party. I often see people I haven't seen since last summer's party. This year the party took place a few weeks following my session with Dave and Diane and I was curious to see if they had continued with the program on their own and if it was helping them with their re-tirement plans.

When we arrived, my wife joined an old friend and I made my way over to join Dave and Diane.

As I approached I heard Dave say, "Here's the guy I was telling you about. I'll introduce you."

Dave introduced me to Lynn who recently moved into the neighborhood and explained they were talking about the session at his house a few weeks ago. He also introduced Craig who was re-tired.

Lynn said, "Dave tells me that you help people plan for re-tirement."

"Yes," I replied. "I conduct workshops and I focus on the non-financial side of re-tirement."

If I Had A Million Dollars

"That's interesting," said Lynn.

Dave said, "We've been talking about re-tirement and I told them about your new way of looking at re-tirement, with a dash.

I asked Craig what he did before re-tirement. He said he re-tired a few years ago from the insurance business.

"Well," I asked, "how is re-tirement treating you?"

"It's great," he replied.

"Don't you recognize him?" said Diane. "He's a City Councilor."

"I knew your name sounded familiar," I said. "How did you get into politics?"

"I've been interested in politics for many years and I like to get involved. When I re-tired I thought, what the heck, why not go for it. I love the job actually."

Lynn had a thoughtful look on her face and said, "If I had a million dollars in the bank, I'd re-tire tomorrow."

I had heard this thinking before so I said to Lynn, "I once met a guy who said the exact same thing, but as we talked it was clear his thoughts on re-tiring ran much deeper than an amount of money in the bank."

To expand I said, "Can I ask you a couple of questions, Lynn? Suppose you had a million dollars in the bank."

"That would be nice," she replied.

"Would you really re-tire?"

She thought and with a slight grin said, "I really don't know. The truth is, I sort of have a love/hate thing with my job and re-tirement may be an option."

"When can you re-tire?" I asked.

"I'm a lawyer and with my firm I can re-tire whenever I want. There are some people in our firm who should have re-tired years ago, and maybe I'm one of them. But I'm still plodding away. It's a tough decision. What if I don't like it?"

Lynn asked me at what age most people re-tire and I told her that there is no simple answer to that question. Statistically people are re-tiring younger, but everybody's conditions are different.[6] For some people the decision is made for them by the rules set out in their pension formula or the workplace. For people who have some control over when they can re-tire, it can be a difficult decision because so many factors can come into play.

I asked Lynn if she had any plans for re-tirement.

"Not yet." she replied, "Despite its problems, I still like going to work."

"Then why think about re-tiring?" I asked. "If you don't have to re-tire and if you enjoy your work, there is nothing wrong with staying where you are."

"I realize that," said Lynn. "But a few of my friends have re-tired and I guess it's kind of infectious. One of my closest friends re-tired last year and is having a great time. In fact, I hardly get a chance to see her anymore. And look at Craig, he's having the time of his life."

Craig beamed in agreement, so I asked him how he made the decision to re-tire.

---

6. The median age of retirement in the United States and Canada for men is 62 and for women, 61. (US Department of Labor, Bureau of Labor Statistics, Monthly Labor Review Online, October 2001 and Economica Ltd. The *Expert Witness* Newsletter, Spring 2003 Vol. 8, No. 1 Retirement Trends in Canada, Kelly Rathje)

"I guess it came naturally," he replied. "I've always been interested in politics and quite frankly, I'd been in insurance for so long I was definitely in need of a change. One day I just sat down and said to myself, if not now, when? I guess I'm lucky; the decision was easy to make."

"You are lucky" I said and then turned to Lynn, "Lynn, I can give you some things to think about to help your decision."

"I would really appreciate that," said Lynn.

We sat down and I said, "Let's put re-tirement aside for a moment. Say you had another decision to make, like you wanted to buy a new car. How would you decide on which car was best for you?"

"I would test-drive a few cars to see which one I preferred," said Dave.

"Good idea. What else?"

"You could read consumer reports," said Lynn. "Or talk to people who owned each car to get their impressions. Also, you could look at the resale values and safety reports."

"In other words," I said, "you should do your homework. You should gather, compare and weigh the relevant information. Well, the same process can be applied to the decision to re-tire."

I explained to Lynn that we approach this by looking at satisfying needs from work in re-tirement.

"The first step," I said, "is to gather the relevant information and look at the various factors that can bear on this decision."

I asked, "What information should you gather in making the decision to re-tire? What factors can come into play?"

Lynn said, "Hmmm, I haven't thought about this before.

I suppose if you are having health problems you might want to re-tire. And of course money is important."

"Yes, money and health can influence the decision to re-tire," I replied. "But can you think of anything else?"

"If you didn't like your work you might be anxious to re-tire," said Craig.

"That can be very important," I said. "We could also include family considerations, and the timing of a spouse's re-tirement. I would suggest, however, that there are three main factors to consider in the decision to re-tire."

I looked around, reached for a napkin and wrote the following:

"He loves to write messages," said Dave. "The other day he kept writing on his fence."

I smiled and said, "To make a rational decision about when to re-tire, you have to gather information on these three factors. Push factors include the things you are happy to give up at work, the Pull factors are the things you look forward to in re-tirement, and money is, well, money.

"Let's start with money because the first thing that pops

into most people's minds when they think of when to re-tire is whether or not they will have enough money. In fact, when most people think about re-tirement planning often the only thing they think about is financial planning."

"Having enough money is both a quantitative and qualitative judgment," I explained. "Money is expressed as a quantitative dollar figure such as I need X dollars to re-tire. But 'need' is a qualitative entity and only you can judge when enough is enough. And if you don't know how you will spend your time in re-tirement, it can be difficult to figure out if you have enough money.

"So, when making the decision to re-tire, in addition to looking at how much money you need to re-tire, you also have to ask yourself..."

"Does this question sound familiar?" I asked.

"Sure does," said Dave.

"Your answer to this question represents the qualitative approach to the decision to re-tire. A few years ago it symbolized the feelings of many Baby Boomers about working hard to acquire a home in the suburbs and a bunch of expensive toys. But this nagging question is still pertinent today as the Boomers are on the verge of re-tirement."

"The reason we enjoy any activity is because it satisfies our needs and the secret to re-tirement happiness is to replace needs lost from work. Your re-tirement will be worthwhile and enjoyable if it satisfies your needs, such as being with people, stimulation, routine, power, and so on. Therefore, the question 'Are we having fun yet?' becomes:" I reached for another napkin and wrote....

To put this into practice, I emphasized that gathering the relevant information begins with clarifying your needs and skills and then comparing those that will be met in retirement, to those currently met through work. If this comparison reveals that more needs and skills will be met when you re-tire, then you have an argument in favor of re-tiring. Alternatively, if more of your needs and skills are met now through work, re-tiring now could be a mistake. In Lynn's case, without knowing any more details, it seems that she was not ready for re-tirement.

Push/Pull Comparison

As explained earlier, the Push factors include all the things you would be happy to leave behind when you re-tire; they are pushing you into re-tirement. The Pull considerations include the things you are looking forward to or pulling you into re-tirement.[7]

"By listing your Push and Pull considerations," I explained, "you are gathering more information to help with your decision, so give this serious thought. Don't rush. Take a hard look at the items in both categories. After comparing your Push and Pull factors it may become clear which is the best option. Obviously it would be preferable if you were looking forward to re-tirement and your decision was based mainly on Pull factors. If not, re-tiring may be a case of going from the frying pan to the fire. Having said that, eventually everyone has to re-tire so you had better get to work to redress the balance between your Push and Pull considerations."

"They sound like worthwhile exercises. I'll definitely try them," said Lynn.

"So let me ask you again, Lynn. If you had a million dollars in the bank would you re-tire tomorrow?"

Lynn smiled, "Not until my Pull factors outweighed my Push factors."

---

7. For example, from the Cornell Retirement and Well-Being Study mentioned earlier, reasons for working in retirement included several Push Factors - *didn't like work, not appreciated, older worker policy and job ended* - as well as one Pull Factor - *to do other things.*

Spouses Re-tiring Together

"One thing we've been thinking about," said Dave, "is whether or not Diane and I should re-tire at the same time."

"An important question," I said.

I turned to Lynn and Craig to see if this was a concern. Lynn said she was a single mother so it was not an issue for her, but she was interested to hear what I had to say. Craig said his wife was working.

I said to Dave and Diane, "Some couples prefer to re-tire at the same time, while others do not. This decision involves a number of factors that deserve serious consideration."

I told them a story about a couple from one of my workshops. Cindy was about to re-tire, but was not looking forward to it because she did not want to spend time with her retired (without the dash) husband. It seems that several years ago, Cindy and her husband both retired at the same time. Although they had not discussed this, she took an early retirement from her job to spend time with her husband.

Cindy explained that the day after her husband retired he reached into his job jar and decided to paint the house. He woke up at his usual time and they had breakfast together. Then he went outside to paint the house. At 10:00 he took a break and they had coffee together. Then he went back to painting the house. At 12:00 they had lunch together, at 3:00 he took a coffee break and at 4:30 he quit working.

The next day, he followed the same routine. This went on until he finished painting the house. At that point Cindy thought, great now we can spend some time together. Well, it didn't work out that way. He then rebuilt the garden, and when he ran out of home jobs, he volunteered to help the neighbors fix up their places. Cindy was so disappointed and frustrated that she begged her former employer to have her job back. She was rehired, but now she was coming up to mandatory retirement and was not looking forward to it.

"This is a rather extreme case and I am not suggesting that it has anything to do with you two. However, it touches on several points worth thinking about.

"First, the decision for a couple to re-tire together should not be taken for granted. It requires honest, open dialogue well in advance. It is clear that Cindy and her husband had completely different expectations about how they would spend their re-tirement. She expected to spend time with her husband, while he had different ideas. It is also clear they did not express their feelings about re-tirement before they re-tired. If they had discussed before re-tirement what each thought they would like to do, and if her husband had been honest, as a minimum, Cindy would not have taken an early re-tirement.

"In addition, Cindy and her husband failed to find worthwhile alternatives after retirement (retired without the dash). Her husband seemingly had plenty to do; Cindy, on the other hand, did not have any plans for retirement and was relying on her husband to do things together. Unfortunately, when this failed to materialize, her only consideration was to return to work (she took the easy way out)."

Cindy's husband reminded me of people who soon after re-tirement say they have so much to do, that there just aren't enough hours in the day to do it all. For some people this may be true. Others, I suspect, are filling time with 'busy' work. They lack a Central Life Focus in re-tirement. And when they run out of busy work, problems can set in.

I said to Dave and Diane, "Now is the time for you to start talking about various scenarios for when either or both of you re-tire. Here's what I suggest you do. Both of you should evaluate your re-tirement plans and your current work based on your needs and skills. We did this with your re-tirement plans at your house a few weeks ago. This should identify any omissions in either or both of your plans and will enable you to compare re-tirement with your current work.

"Then think about and list your Push and Pull considerations. If your Push outweighs your Pull list, think about how to reverse this situation to create a re-tirement preferable to being at work. As you do these exercises ask yourselves, 'When does the fun begin?' If you are honest and spend some time with this, the answer you have been searching for just might appear."

"We both have been looking at our plans," said Diane, "Now we'll try these other exercises."

There was a pause and Dave said, "There is one more thing that has been bothering me. I hate to admit it but when I think about re-tiring it's like I'm getting old. Know what I mean? I don't want people to think of me as a senior citizen. It scares me."

"I feel exactly the same way Dave," said Lynn. "I know it's silly, but some things you just can't deny."

"You are touching on a very important topic that is near and dear to my heart," I replied. "I say this because I have spent many years teaching re-tirement education and although this concern is common, it is completely misplaced. My concern is, if you believe that re-tirement is somehow connected to ageing or growing old, and this is a common belief, it can have negative consequences. Of course we are getting older; but this has absolutely nothing to do with re-tirement. Unfortunately most people, including many who write books and run courses on retirement, do not understand this issue.

"Before we get into that subject," I said, "one of my immediate needs is to get some more of that delicious potato salad. Then I'll show you a completely different way to look at the issue of ageing and re-tirement. I'm not trying to sweep this under the carpet hoping it will go away. I just want to show you that your concern about growing old and re-tirement is unwarranted and harmful. Be right back."

Chapter Highlights

- There is more to the decision to re-tire than money considerations.
- Start by gathering the appropriate information including your Push factors - things you are happy to give up at work, and Pull factors - things you look forward to in re-tirement.
- Ask yourself when will you be able to satisfy your needs? The freedom of re-tirement just happens to be the perfect opportunity to maximize the satisfaction of your needs.
- Compare needs and skills that will be met in re-tirement to those currently met through work.
- Compare your Push and Pull lists.
- Couples re-tiring together should discuss re-tirement plans together and apart, well in advance of re-tirement.

Retired Teachers Research Results

Ninety-four per cent of respondents indicated that they retired by choice. Reasons for retiring, however, varied considerably.

Reason for retiring:

Felt it was time to retire	51%
Wanted to do other things besides work	38%
Retirement income sufficient to do so	34%
Wanted more time for self and family	32%
Unhappy with work situation	23%
Spouse retired then	15%
Health reasons	8%
Not performing job up to my expectations	4%

Addition reasons included:

I was "drained"
U.S. Govt. offered job teaching overseas
Youth needed teaching job
I own my own company
Scared
Could make as much with retirement as working.
My program was cut
Need to take care of elderly mother
Tired - "burned out"
Forced out its older faculty from the college of medicine
Became caregiver for husband

Teacher burnout—early buyout
Spouse was retired, and I wanted to work part time
Stress
Wanted to pursue other career options
Wanted to leave on a high note while I still liked teaching
Took a job outside teaching field
Maximum age and years to retire to get the best benefits
Mental Health!
Burned out
Not adequately compensated for work /ability
Loss of son in accident
Wanted to move
Financial incentives from district and state
Pressure from parents concerning their child
Weary, and just felt it was time to leave

Although most retired by choice, those who did not retire by choice gave the following reasons for retiring.

Health reasons	69%
Burnout	54%
Reached mandatory retirement age	23%
Was forced by administration	8%
Budget cutbacks	8%

Additional reasons included:

Did not like Administration and staying longer had no effect on retirement income.
Too many hassles
Program was cut
I felt I was running out of steam for my children
Spouse request
I realized it was time to start smelling the roses
Negative behaviors of students
Unhappy with teen-age problems; drugs, etc.

"There was pressure in the form of perception of others - older teachers should retire to give young ones jobs - young people have new ideas, etc. I believe many schools have been decapitated - all of the experience has walked out the door. Many of the "new" ideas were new to earlier generations of teachers once, too."

When asked if they could do it over again if they would still retire at the same age, they responded:

Retire at same age	70%
Retire at younger age	4%
Retire at older age	15%
Not certain	11%

(Continued)

Lesson Learned

Although ninety-five percent retired by choice, there are many underlying factors that can contribute to this choice. Some relate to 'Push' factors, such as being unhappy with the work situation, forced by administration, budget cutbacks, student behavior, stress, burnout, etc. Others related to 'Pull' factors such as wanting to do other things, spouse retiring, and family caregiving.

There may be things beyond your control that may force you to retire. If so, it is extremely important that you apply the techniques provided by the Road Map to ensure that you are able to take part in new activities that will replace satisfactions lost from work.

8

When I'm Sixty-Four

(*The Beatles, 1967*)

I have spent over 20 years studying, researching, writing about, and teaching the re-tirement experience. This includes many years teaching Social Gerontology (the study of ageing) and working with thousands of pre and post-re-tirees through my workshops. Based on this experience I have come to the conclusion that in the context of re-tirement, a discussion on ageing is both irrelevant and detrimental. It is irrelevant because ageing has nothing to do with re-tirement, and it is detrimental because it can reinforce the commonly held misconception that when one retires, one is getting old. This may have applied to generations of retirees in that past, but it most certainly does not apply today, especially with people re-tiring so young. So pervasive is this issue that I feel compelled to clear up a few misconceptions.

Technically, the ageing process begins at birth. It is common, however, to use the term ageing to refer to growing older and to make the connection between ageing in the context of growing older, and re-tirement. Reinforced by the structure of private and public pension schemes, to my mind it is wrong to base the point of re-tirement primarily on age. Having said that, if we must use age to expedite re-tirement and calculate pension rates, we must not assume that re-tirement is related to ageing or getting old. If you believe this, you are guilty of what I call the 'ageist's self-fulfilling prophecy'.

I returned with a bowl of potato salad, sat down and said. "When we talked about re-tirement and ageing, you said you were concerned about people thinking of you as old. Unfortunately this feeling is not uncommon and it is tied into the traditional image of retirement (without the dash) I discussed earlier with Dave. The problem is most people make this connection because it has always been part of thinking about retirement, and coincidently, we tend to be older when we re-tire. The heart of the matter is wrapped up in the concept called the self-fulfilling prophecy. That is, if we believe something strongly, even if it isn't accurate, we tend to act in ways that are consistent with that expectation."

In the first chapter I included an example of the salesman and the missing jack as an example of the self-fulfilling prophecy. The salesman defined his situation (needing a jack) in such a way (being overcharged) that he no longer wanted what he originally set out to get.[8]

Ageist Self-Fulfilling Prophecy

After briefly describing the self-fulfilling prophecy, I said, "The same situation can take place with respect to ageing and re-tirement. For example, I met a person in my work-

8. Originally conceptualized by Robert Merton in the 1950s, the self-fulfilling prophecy occurs when a false definition of the situation evokes a new behavior, which makes the original false conception come true.

shop who truly believed that he would not live very long after he re-tired. This was pretty extreme thinking and obviously I was quite surprised to hear him say this, so I asked how long his parents lived. His mother was 82 and was still alive. His father lived to be over 80. Clearly there was no biological reason for his belief. But the problem was he so firmly held on to this belief that he may help to bring it about.

"This man was a victim of what I call the Ageist Self-fulfilling Prophecy. An ageist is to older people as a racist is to certain ethnic groups, and a sexist is to women. Ageism implies prejudice or discrimination against or negative attitudes toward people based on their age. For our purposes, the Ageist Self-fulfilling Prophecy simply means that if you believe that when you re-tire you will be old, or that others will think of you that way, you may look for signs to prove or validate your belief and if you look hard enough, you will find them even if you have to create them.

To give an example that they could relate to I asked, "Do any of you know of someone who passed away soon after re-tirement?"

A solemn hush fell over the group. This is a serious matter. After all, these people are about to re-tire and the implications behind this thought are pretty scary.

Diane said to Dave, "What about Alex? Didn't he die about a year after he re-tired?"

"Yes, he did," Dave replied. "And he wasn't that much older than me. It makes you wonder."

With a somber face I replied, "Terrible isn't it?" I paused to let this thought sink in.

Then I said, "Now let me ask, does anyone know someone who recently re-tired and who is still alive?"

It took a few seconds for this thought to register and when it did the tone changed from gloom to laughter and relief.

"Our mind does funny things," I said. "If we hear of someone who dies soon after re-tirement, this sticks in our mind. We think re-tirement killed him or her. But we don't think about the millions of people who may actually live longer because they re-tired. Also, there is no way to test if Alex would still be alive if he did not re-tire. Once somebody re-tires and dies, you can't bring him or her back to see if they would live longer by not re-tiring. Yet if we hear about someone dying soon after re-tirement, the ageist self-fulfilling prophecy leads us to falsely believe that re-tirement killed them."

Memory And Ageing

Another common example of the Ageist's Self Fulfilling Prophecy is memory loss. To emphasize this I said, "Let me ask you another question. Do you find that as you get older, and I am not denying that we are getting older, that you are starting to forget things, like people's names, or where you left your keys?"

"Would you repeat the question?" said Craig. "I forget what you were asking."

They all laughed at Craig's comment but I suspect deep down it was a nervous laugh and that they could relate to this problem.

I started to repeat my question, stopped and said, "Seriously, if you find that you are starting to forget things, is it logical to conclude that you are getting old?"

There was silence, so I went on to say, "I have some

good news and some bad news. The bad news is if you believe that forgetting things is a sign of your age, you are a victim of the Ageist Self-fulfilling Prophecy. The good news is, forgetting things as you get older is not necessarily a result of your age."

"What else could it be?" asked Lynn.

"I will explain that in a minute," I replied.

"I admit that as people get older there is one very important thing they start to forget. I am not talking about forgetting where you put your car keys or a person's name. These are minor compared to what I am referring to."

I went on to ask, "Can anybody tell me, what is the most significant thing that people forget as they get older?"

"I think forgetting a person's name is pretty significant," said Lynn.

"It's only significant if you see it as a sign of ageing," I said. "Besides, not everyone starts to forget people's names as they get older and in a moment I will show you that it is not a sign of ageing."

Again I asked them what people forget as they get older, and again, I did not get a response. So I answered my own question. "The most important thing that people forget as they get older, is that they used to forget things when they were younger."

I paused to let this sink in.

"And more importantly," I continued, "when you were 22 and forgot something you just accepted the fact that you had a bad memory.

"But now when you forget things you interpret it as a sign of ageing. Secretly at the back of your mind you think, oh my God, I must be getting senile, or have Alzheimer's disease.

"This is the natural conclusion of false logic (or a false definition of the situation). If you start with the assumptions that old people forget things and that re-tirees are old, and you start to forget things, the logical conclusion is, I must be getting old. You define the situation as real; look for clues to confirm it - like forgetting something - and it becomes real in its consequence. You reinforce the connection between re-tirement and growing old."

To elaborate on this sensitive issue I told them about research on memory and ageing and that it generally supports the assumption that as people grow older their short-term memory diminishes.

"The problem is," I said, "most of this research is based on the Ageist Self-fulfilling Prophecy. To explain what I mean, I can describe a piece of research I designed to look at the effects of height on short-term memory. I believe that short people have better short-term memory than tall people."

They looked a bit surprised by this assertion so I went on to say, "Before jumping to any conclusions about my sanity, I am using a tongue-in-cheek example to make a point.

"To test my hypothesis that short people have better short-term memory than tall people, suppose I asked everyone at this street party to line up from the shortest to the tallest and then I divided them into two groups based on their height. Then suppose I gave each person a short-term memory test to recall a number of objects after a 15-minute interval.

"Now let's suppose that on average, the short people did marginally better than the tall people in recalling the objects. Voila, I have confirmed my original hypothesis. Short-term memory is affected by a person's height."

They all looked at me in disbelief. To take this to the next level, I asked if my conclusion made sense.

"Of course not," said Lynn. "It's silly. Everyone knows that memory has nothing to do with a person's height."

"Also," said Diane, "you are only looking at people from this party. And you have to admit they are a pretty weird group."

"OK," I responded. "Let's continue with Lynn's thought. If it doesn't make sense that memory is affected by height, how else can we explain why my research found that short people have superior short-term memory?"

"I don't know," said Diane.

"My background is in Sociology," I said. "Sociologists are interested in explaining attitudes, belief systems and behavior based in part on the social structure or social groups a person belongs to. So as a Sociologist I might conclude that short people tend to sit in the front of the classroom and they are more likely to be asked a question by the teacher. To prepare for this eventuality, they develop short-term memory skills."

"That doesn't make sense either," said Diane.

"I agree," I said, "So let's try a different approach. What explanation would a psychologist who is interested in personality development come up with to explain our height and memory findings? Don't be shy. If my sociological explanation is ridiculous, can anybody explain the difference in short-term memory based on different personalities? Give me a tongue-in-cheek explanation to explain why short people have better short-term memory than tall people."

"Short people have to compensate for their lack of height," said Diane.

"That's a good explanation," I replied. "It's often referred to as the Napoleon Syndrome."

Lynn suggested that women, who tend to be shorter, have superior brains.

"Excellent," I said. "We have come up with several quite different and admittedly silly explanations to explain why short people perform better on a memory test compared to tall people.

"Now let's look again at the real world and the research on memory and age. I have looked at some of this research and in general it supports the assumption that age has a negative effect on short-term memory. Interestingly, age seems to have a positive effect on long-term memory, but that is another issue. The main issue is that when researchers compare two different groups of people who differ by age, and when they find differences in memory scores, they assume that these differences were caused by age differences. I, for one, question this assumption."

To carry this thought forward I asked, "Can anyone think of another explanation, other than age, that might explain why older people do not do as well on short-term memory tests?"

This caused a moment of silence and then Craig said, "Is it because our brains have more information; we have more to remember?"

"I'm afraid not," I replied. "Apparently we are only using 14% of our brain, so there is plenty of room left."

To give them a hint, I asked, "When somebody does research on memory and age, where do you think the young subjects in this research came from?"

"The university, they're students," Dave said.

"Of course. And what are university students supposed to devote their time to? Studying, naturally. So we find that in all cases the young people who take part in this research are university students who spend most of their time exercising their short-term memory. Besides, students are used to writing exams and do not feel intimidated by researchers in lab coats. No wonder they do better on short-term memory tests.

"The older subjects, on the other hand, do not exercise their short-term memory as often or as intensely as the younger students, and many are not as comfortable in a research situation.

"It is quite possible that you are starting to forget things as you get older. However, the reason is not necessarily the ageing process or mind deterioration. It is because you do not exercise your short-term memory as much as you used to."

I went on to explain, "When you were younger and just starting out, you were learning new things every day. You were learning how to perform your job, meeting new people, remembering which child wants what sandwich in their lunch, remembering when to take the children to hockey practice, piano lessons, and so on. As time passes, when the job becomes second nature and the children leave home, your short-term memory can begin to coast.

"As with most bodily functions," I continued, "short-term memory is a function of use. The adage, 'use it or lose it' applies just as readily to short-term memory as to muscle strength. I have met people who returned to school after their children have grown. When asked if their short-term memory had improved, without exception they told me that it improved significantly. The reason it improved is because they were beginning to exercise their short-term memory.

"If you find that you are starting to forget things, you

have several options. You can get involved in activities that will exercise your short-term memory, such as going back to school, joining a theater group where you have to memorize lines, or you can memorize the phone book. These exercises will definitely improve your short-term memory. Alternatively, and this is my preference, you can stop worrying or blaming your age and just accept what is happening - you are not exercising your short-term memory as much as you used to.[9]

"I am not denying that in some cases, elderly people experience memory loss due to physiological changes or problems. My point is that when short-term memory begins to fail it should not be construed as a sign that you are getting old or senile. People who worry about their memory convince themselves that there is something wrong and that it relates to growing old, or to being re-tired. Re-tirement can affect short-term memory only if your mind stagnates."

The self-fulfilling prophecy is not always working in a negative direction.

"The beauty of the self-fulfilling prophecy," I continued, "is it can work for you, rather than against you. If you truly believe, and you should, that re-tirement is like winning a lottery, and that you will find worthwhile and enjoyable pursuits, you have a far better chance of succeeding. Don't get bogged down with the Ageist Self-fulfilling Prophecy and

---

9. In a recent study of nearly 3000 people aged 65 to 94, those given 10 hours of training in memory, problem-solving, and decision making tasks over the course of several weeks showed marked and lasting increases in cognitive ability. 'Booster' training sessions received a year later resulted in further improvement in mental function which persisted for over a year. (American Academy of Anti-Aging Medicine, The World Health Network, Keeping Ageing Brains On top Form)

don't look for signs to confirm that you are getting old. Instead, look for signs to confirm your advantageous situation. You will find them; they are everywhere."

Midlife Crisis Re-defined

I turned my attention to Lynn and asked, "If you don't mind my asking, how old are you Lynn?"

She smiled, hesitated, and said, "No, I don't mind. I'm fifty-two."

"The reason I asked is I get the impression that your concerns are not solely directed toward re-tirement."

"Well, I guess that's true," she said. "The problem is my life feels sort of flat now. I have a good law practice and things are going well. But, I don't know. Something is missing. That's why when Dave mentioned re-tirement it perked my interest. I realize now that just having money is not enough. I have to find alternatives to keep me busy. But it's true. I probably won't re-tire for a few years yet."

"It sounds to me, Lynn, that you may be experiencing what some people refer to as a mid-life crisis."

"You may be right," she replied.

"In that case, I would be happy to share my views on this issue. They may give you a new way of making sense of this problem. And even though your re-tirement is a few years away, it might just turn out to be a cure for this malaise."

"OK," said Lynn.

There has been a great deal of research on the so-called mid-life crisis and volumes have been written on it. Through my workshop experience I have developed a few insights that I wanted to share with Lynn and the others. Admittedly, my approach and analysis is somewhat simplistic, but I felt it could shed some light on an issue that can be misunderstood.

So, in response to Lynn's concern I said, "One way to look at the middle-age crisis is to view it as the 'systematic elimination of unanswered questions and goals'. This may sound somewhat formal but to understand this, think back to when you were much younger. At that time, your future was infinite. You had everything to look forward to and your head was full of questions and expectations about what your future held. I am sure you wondered: if, when, and who you would marry; how many children you would have; what they would be like; where you would live; what type of work you would pursue; how rich you would be; and so on. Your head was full of unanswered questions about what might lie ahead in your future. The last thing on your mind was re-tirement."

"Suddenly you have reached a point in your life where most of your unanswered questions have been answered - some to your satisfaction and others not to your satisfaction. You know if and whom you would marry, how rich you would be, and so on. The only major unanswered question that lies ahead is re-tirement, the last thing on your mind when you were younger. If you are not totally satisfied with some aspect of your life and you feel that it is too late to make any changes, if your life no longer includes many unanswered questions or goals, and the thought of re-tiring scares you, do not lose heart. Re-tirement can be your saving grace."

To take a more critical look at middle age, what exactly does the term imply? To my mind it suggests a mid-point in the progression from birth to death. This image portrays life as linear suggesting that it follows a straight line based on a single dimension - age. Also, by focusing on a mid-point between birth and death, it implies that the second half will involve losses and that it will not be as good as the first half. Middle age is halfway to the end. No wonder it can be scary.

The good news is this description is not totally accurate. Life experiences from the past and into the future are not linear and are not based solely on age. People are not one-dimensional. Our incomes, levels of education, individual skills, confidence levels, family status, net worth, to name but a few, change over the lifespan and will continue to change into the future. At certain points, any one of these dimensions may be on the rise, on a level plane, or on the decline. We are the gestalt of our experiences.

The Centerpoint

"I am not denying that life can be quite different when you re-tire. However, to more accurately reflect the process of transition, I suggest rather than identifying a mid-point between life and death, we focus on what I call the 'Centerpoint' of life.

"The Centerpoint is when the individual re-tires with a dash, changes from a work to a re-tirement career, and gets a 'new set of wheels'. Portrayed as a central point rather than mid way between two points, you can go off in any direction. It involves drawing on past experiences to plan a new career that encompasses the best of their work and leisure careers. It doesn't matter how long you take to process the fusion of your work and leisure careers, the important point is the benefits gained through the process. If you have an exciting re-tirement to look forward to, or are experiencing a re-tirement that is worthwhile and enjoyable, you have re-introduced a series of goals and unanswered questions to your life. In so doing, you will either not experience, or at least minimize, the mid-life crisis."

My reference to the Centerpoint is not simply a marketing ploy (like a retirement home). It is a more accurate way to describe the convergence of your work and leisure careers. This new concept did not exist for past generations because they were less likely to be able to step back and plan for their life following their working career. Re-tirees today are lucky to have this opportunity. Also, you do not have to be re-tired to begin this planning process. In fact, it is preferable that it begins well in advance of re-tirement.

"I encourage you," I continued, "to look upon this period of your life not as middle-age, but as a staging point and the ideal opportunity to prepare yourself for your re-tirement career. Use this opportunity to re-introduce unanswered questions and goals to your life. Your unanswered questions and goals for the future will probably be quite different from those that you eliminated up to this point. For the future, you may wonder how you can apply some of your knowledge and skills to benefit others, how you can satisfy your needs and skills through different activities, how your re-tirement career will unfold, and so on. If you re-introduce questions and goals to your life, you will replace your malaise with optimism."

I had spoken at length about an issue that I felt was very important. To see if my arguments hit home, I asked Dave, "Well, have I convinced you that re-tirement has nothing to do with growing old?"

"You have," said Dave. "I can see that just because one is re-tired, it doesn't mean that you are old. I really didn't stop to think of it that way."

"Hearing what you have to say," said Diane, "especially the part about the self-fulfilling prophecy, makes me feel younger."

"That's great," I replied.

"Like I mentioned to Dave a few weeks ago, you should consider yourselves lucky to be re-tiring now rather than in the past."

"I remember," said Dave. "You said that re-tiring Baby Boomers should be called the Luckies."

"That's right," I replied. "From Hippies, to Yuppies to Luckies."

"What do you mean by that?" Lynn asked.

The Future For The Boomers

"Well, consider how you differ from retirees in the past. Dave and I discussed this a few weeks ago. But in a nutshell, as I am sure you are aware, the Boomers have many advantages compared to past generations of retirees. On average, they will be richer, live longer, be more educated, and will expect more from life.

"But another advantage is that society's image of retirement is changing for the better, and this in turn will influence your self-image as a re-tiree. Re-tirement is becoming something to be proud of. So, considering how things have improved, I would say you are lucky to be re-tiring now rather than a generation or two ago. That is why I suggest we refer to re-tiring Baby Boomers as the Luckies."

"I guess you are right," said Lynn. "When I look at my parents' or grandparents' generation, things are definitely better now."

"And who knows what the future holds," I added. "Things may not be as good for future generations of re-tirees. So you are definitely lucky to be re-tiring now."

I wanted to explain a point I mentioned a few minutes ago so I said, "Probably one of the biggest changes in what I call the new re-tirement, is the change in society's attitude toward re-tirement. And this is based mainly on economic considerations."

I explained that each segment of society develops and retains a sense of self-importance, or lack of importance, in part, due to its economic buying power. Clearly, pre-Boomer retirees were not significant in terms of numbers, they did not live very long after retirement, and they did not have economic clout. They simply did not represent a market large enough to be pursued by the providers of goods and services. Advertising aimed at older people in the past generally focused on health aids and other age related entities. TV in the past rarely included retired people and if they were included they were portrayed negatively. It was as though they did not exist.

"But things will be different when you re-tire," I said. "You represent a huge identifiable market that the suppliers of clothing, entertainment, cosmetics, food, cars, motorcycles, travel, to name but a few, will continue to court especially in re-tirement. When the Boomers were younger, to attract their attention, advertising agencies portrayed happy, lively, healthy, sexy, young people enjoying whatever it was they had to sell. This reinforced the Boomers self-image of being the most advantageous group in society. Do you remember the phrase 'never trust anyone over 30'? This arrogance reflected a sense of self-importance that was spawned by the economic power of the Boomers when they were young. It was easy to feel proud of being a Hippie and a Yuppie because they held economic and political power.

"The beauty of re-tiring now is the Boomers will retain

their political and economic clout into re-tirement and the suppliers of goods and services will continue to court them with vigor. As a result, re-tirees will be portrayed differently from the past. They will be seen as happy, lively, healthy, sexy, older people enjoying whatever the advertisers wish to sell."

I told them to think of the significance of this major shift and how it will affect society's image of re-tirement. When the Boomers re-tire they will consist of millions of people with nothing but time and money on their hands and they are just itching to find happiness that eluded many of them while they were at work. I am willing to bet the barn that the image of re-tirement is in for a dramatic change.

"The signs are everywhere," I said. "For example, why do you think the major clothing manufacturers introduced loose fitting or relaxed jeans a few years ago? Do you think this is simply a fashion statement? When I was a kid, loose fitting jeans were called 'huskies'. If you had to buy huskies it meant you couldn't fit into regular fitting jeans. Today, clothing manufacturers want to continue selling to us but many of us need huskies and the word huskies is not very flattering. To overcome this conundrum, the manufacturers simply repackaged huskies as relaxed fitting. The product is the same; only the name and its image have changed."

"I know of another example," said Lynn. "Up until a few years ago, every winter my son and I drove to Florida. It became a routine that we stopped at a particular fast food restaurant. A few years ago, we stopped at the restaurant and the area that used to be called Play Land was divided in half. Now they had the play area for the kids on one side and a player piano on the other side."

"That's a good example," I said. "Clearly the fast food industry has realized the importance of older Boomers as customers and has begun to accommodate their interests. This is the tip of the iceberg. We see the popularity of music from the 60's and 70's. If you flip through the radio dial it seems as though there are as many stations playing the hits from the past as those playing today's music. And if you check the newsstand you will find many new magazines that cater to re-tirees. This was unheard of in the past."

"That makes a lot of sense," said Lynn. "But it may be easier said than done."

Dave said to Lynn, "Diane and I went through your Life Goal Planning program with our friends a few weeks ago. It has definitely given me some guidance and I am beginning to see more clearly what I can do when I re-tire."

"It's never too early to begin thinking about how you will spend your time and how to satisfy your needs and skills in re-tirement," I said.

At that point, Dave's grandson came over and pulled him away from the discussion. As the party was beginning to break up, I excused myself and withdrew to find my wife. As I left I said, "Don't forget now, keep buying those relaxed jeans."

Chapter Summary

- The Ageist Self-Fulfilling Prophecy means that if you believe that when you re-tire you are getting old, you will look for signs to prove or validate your belief. If you look hard enough you will find them, even if you have to create them.

- The self-fulfilling prophecy can work for you, rather than against you. If you truly believe that re-tirement is like winning a lottery and that you will find enjoyable and worthwhile pursuits, you have a far better chance that this will come true.

- The Mid-Life Crisis is characterized as the point when most of your goals and unanswered questions have been eliminated, and if you are not entirely satisfied with your life, and feel it is too late to make changes, a crisis might ensue. The problem with this explanation is it portrays life as linear and that mid-life is somewhere between birth and death.

- A more accurate description is the Centerpoint of life. This is when the individual changes from a work to a re-tirement career, and draws on past experiences to plan a new career. In so doing, you can re-introduce goals and unanswered questions to your life.

- In so far as the economic and political strength of the Boomers will accompany them into re-tirement, the marketing focus and society's attitude toward re-tirement will change in a positive direction.

9

With A Little Help From My Friends

(*The Beatles, 1967*)

The phone rang in my office and it was Janice. "I don't know if you remember me," she said, "but my husband Les and I met you at Dave and Diane's house a month ago."

"Of course I remember you, Janice. What can I do for you?" I asked.

She confessed that she was having a problem with Les. She sounded worried and I asked her to explain.

"I didn't want to talk about this at Diane's house," she said, "but Les has changed completely since he retired a year ago. I don't know what to do. And he is talking about moving but I'm not sure I want to go."

"How has he changed, Janice?" I asked.

"He is making my life miserable by hanging over my neck 24 hours a day. He criticizes my cooking; he has to go grocery shopping with me and decide on everything I put in the cart. When the phone rings, he runs to answer, although no one ever calls him, and he stands around while I talk. Last summer we had a lovely lawn with flowerbeds. He dug up everything and planted a vegetable garden. We had vegetables coming out of our ears. Then he got upset because I wouldn't preserve it all. I don't know what to do. I'm at my wits end."[10]

After listening, I suggested we take this one step at a time.

"What do you think the problem is?" I asked.

"I don't know," she replied. "But it's serious."

"If you think back to what we talked about at Diane's house," I said, "it seems to me that the problem is really quite obvious. Les is looking desperately for something to do; he's bored. And to make matters worse, he is interfering with your life and activities. In other words, he is trying to replace satisfactions lost from work through his home and your activities. He tried being a cook, shopper, telephone operator, and a gardener. But these activities have not brought him happiness."

"I couldn't agree with you more," said Janice. "But what can we do?"

I had a few suggestions I felt could help, but thought it best to include Les in the discussion. So I suggested they both meet at my office the following week to discuss how Les's re-tirement was progressing and his thoughts about moving. Janice was delighted.

The following week I began the conversation by asking Les how re-tirement was progressing. He told me that he was starting to apply some of my exercises and that he was thinking about moving. I took this as my cue and asked where he was planning to move.

---

10. I am not making this up. The description of Les's behavior are adaptations of a letter that appeared in a nationally syndicated advice column several years ago.

"Janice and I love the outdoors, so we were thinking about moving west to be near the mountains."

"You mean 'you' were thinking about moving," Janice said to Les. "I told Les the other day, I'm really not sure that I would be happy leaving here. We have our friends and our daughter and her family live here."

"But if we move," Les responded, "we can be closer to Richard and his family. Actually, there are a few things Janice and I are trying to come to grips with since I re-tired. Moving is just one of them."

"The biggest problem," Janice said to me, "is Les is always underfoot. I keep telling him to try to find something else to do, but it doesn't seem to work."

Les responded, "I admit that I've been spending a fair amount of time at home. But some of my best friends are still working."

"Loss of friendships can present problems," I said. "And there's no question re-tirement can affect the marriage relationship. So if you'd like, I can go over some points worth thinking about on this issue."

"I think that would be a good idea," said Janice.

"So do I," said Les. "But, is this a common problem?"

"I wouldn't say it's common," I replied. "But re-tirement can change the ground rules in a marriage and so it's very important to spend a little time thinking about the amount and quality of time you spend together."

I explained that when a family is young, most of the leisure time spent together is with the children. With time, as the children grow up and leave home and the husband and or wife re-tire, the daily rhythm of time together and apart is likely to change. With time no longer occupied by work, an adjustment in the amount of time a couple spends together may be necessary.

Communication

"One of the most important things," I explained, "is communication; true communication is crucial when it comes to planning for re-tirement."

Obviously I had no idea of the inner workings of their marriage, so I spoke in general terms and shared an example from a workshop. We were discussing housing and I asked for a show of hands from those people thinking about moving after re-tirement. Several people raised their hand including one man whose wife turned to him and said in surprise, 'I didn't know we were thinking of moving!'

Janice and Les both smiled and I said, "It's fairly safe to assume that this couple was not communicating about retirement."

"But Janice and I have talked about moving," said Les.

"I realize that," I replied. "My main point is, communication around re-tirement plans is vital because it is a shared experience and the more you know of each other's feelings, the more likely the transition will go smoothly. So sit down together and clarify your feelings. Talk about how you plan to spend your time; what you plan to do apart and what you plan to do together. You may not have immediate answers to these questions, but it is important to start thinking and talking."

I asked Janice, "When you talked to Les about this problem, were you criticizing him or discussing a solution to the problem?"

"I don't know the solution," she replied. "So I guess

I've been criticizing him. We tried to talk after the session with you but we didn't get very far."

"That's OK," I said. "It's a start and Les may have felt frustrated by his situation and found it difficult to talk about. I have a suggestion that may help, but first let's take a look at Janice's concern that you are interfering with her domain."

"That's a good way to put it," said Janice.

Respect Each Other's Territory

I said to Les, "Let me ask you a question. Suppose you were still working. How would you feel if Janice came to work with you and, the first day on the job, began to criticize and tell you how to do things better?"

Les managed a smile but did not answer my question. When I ask this in my workshop, you can imagine it hits the nail right on the head and usually ignites a lively discussion.

To further emphasize my point, I told them the story of Howard. He was happily re-tired, involved in civic duties, and loved to spend time in his basement workshop. One day when his wife was out, he decided to rearrange the kitchen to make it more efficient.

When his wife came home, she never said a word. Howard assumed that she was pleased with his interior design skills. Later, when he was out for the day, his wife rearranged his workshop the way she thought it should be arranged.

"Although Howard's wife did not say anything," I said, "her message was clear - don't touch my stuff.

"Les, I'm not suggesting that you should steer clear of housework, cooking or shopping – sharing these activities in re-tirement can be a blessing for both partners. But if this has traditionally been Janice's domain, then I suggest you discuss your interest in taking on certain tasks with Janice. Sit down and rationally examine the extent to which Janice would feel comfortable with this. Let's face it Les, I imagine Janice has done a great job until now. Just because you're re-tired, doesn't necessarily mean you can interfere.

"To come up with a solution," I said, "you have to understand the problem."

"The problem is clear," said Janice, "Les is interfering with my life."

I asked Les, "Would you agree that this is an accurate assessment of the problem?"

"I suppose so," he responded.

"Then the solution is for you to find other interests; as we discussed before, you have to find activities that will enable you to replace satisfactions lost from work. And, I might add, that do not interfere with Janice's life. Would you say that would solve the problem?" I asked.

"Most definitely," said Janice.

"Les?" I asked.

"I guess so," he replied. "But, one thing I love is playing bridge and I'd love it if Janice joined me. She tried it but she really doesn't like it. I think that might solve part of the problem, but I can't seem to convince her to try."

"Les," I asked, "what do you think the chances are of Janice enjoying bridge after you re-tire, if she didn't like it before? What does your re-tirement have to do with it?"

"I don't know," said Les. "I was just hoping she would like it."

"Am I correct in assuming you're a pretty good bridge player and Janice is a beginner?" I asked. "If so, that may be part of the reason she didn't like it."

"That's true," replied Les. "But she didn't even want to take lessons."

"Well, there's your answer. You have to face the fact that Janice does not share your love of bridge, and your retiring will not change her feelings on this."

"I guess you're right. There's nothing I can do," Les lamented.

"Actually there is something you can do," I said. "You just mentioned two needs you would like to satisfy when you re-tire. One is to continue playing bridge, and the other is to have Janice join you. You may have to continue playing bridge without her. But your desire to share a re-tirement activity with Janice can flourish – just through a different activity. Re-tirement gives you the freedom to develop a new activity together, something you are both starting at the ground floor.

"You can approach this the way I showed you at Dave and Diane's house. You each should take a look at the other's Needs and Skills List and develop a combined list that includes needs and skills that apply to both of you. Then brainstorm an activity you can both take part in."

I explained further, "Of course you two may still have a few things to work out, but eventually you should find that the freedom of re-tirement will enhance your relationship. The bottom line though, Les, is you have to start applying the tools I've given you. You can't rely on Janice to pick up where work left off. It's not fair, and in all likelihood, it's not possible."

Friendships

I wanted to pick up on a statement Les made earlier so I

said, "Les, you mentioned that one of your problems is that some of your friends are still working?"

"Yes," he replied. "I have to admit I miss going to work and seeing my friends."

"That's understandable," I said. "You've spent quite a bit of time at work and probably made quite a few good friends. These are people you saw almost daily, and you share common experiences and stories. On the other hand, there may be people at work who you are happy to never see again. In any case, when work experience is the basis of a common bond, when this is no longer present as in re-tirement, friend-ships can be affected."

"The question that many people must face," I explained, "is what might become of their friendship when they re-tire? For example, when you are out of the picture you are not aware of many changes in the workplace and how these may affect the nature of your friendship. You may know of some-one who re-tired and continues to show up at work just to keep up with what is happening there."

"I used to do that," admitted Les.

"It is also possible," I said, "that if you and a friend from work re-tired at the same time, your re-tirement careers may develop in different directions."

"I suppose that's true," said Les.

If you find that many of your friends are centered on work, or if work is a main interest in your life - which is common - you may have to make an extra effort to find a replacement for those people and interests when you re-tire.

"The main point," I said to Les and Janice, "is that now may be a good time to solidify your present friendships and to expand your friendship circle. For some people this won't present a problem. But for others, it's easier said than done. So, extend yourselves a little. Take some risks; seek people out. This ties nicely with Les's search for re-tirement activities. You'll meet new people when you join a club, take a community college course, or volunteer. Do whatever it takes to get in touch with new people, your source for companionship, support, approval, security, encouragement, and affection. You never know what will come out of this until you try."

- Couples should focus on three key issues - communication, respecting each other's domain, and understanding what the re-tired person is going through in terms of giving up satisfactions lost from work.

- Re-tirement can affect friendships, especially if your friends are still at work.

- It is also possible that if you and a friend from work both re-tired, your re-tirement careers could develop in different directions.

- Re-tirement is a good time to solidify present friendships and to expand your friendship circle.

10

Our House

(*Graham Nash, 1970*)

It was time to take a look at Janice's other concern - moving. This is a common issue in the retirement (without the dash) literature. The problem is the more traditional approach seems to miss the most important elements of this issue. For instance, it is common to focus on the pros and cons of various types of housing (e.g. condominiums, apartments, co-ops, mobile homes, retirement communities, and so on). I call this the real estate approach. This issue may be important, but it ignores the more critical issues, like the one faced by Janice and Les, in the context of changing from a work to a re-tirement career. Their concern goes beyond the real estate issue.

Not everyone wants to move at re-tirement. Many people prefer to stay where they are and have no desire to move at all. Having said that, re-tirement can trigger a housing move. In fact, it can be the perfect time to change your housing situation. Many people at our workshop actively consider moving after they re-tire. Some think about moving to a small town or the cottage; others think about moving back to their place of birth. Many plan to spend the winter months in a warmer climate, while others plan to move to a different –

usually smaller – home within the same city or community. I even met a couple at a workshop who built a bigger home in re-tirement. Everyone has different needs and priorities and it is clear that the decision to move goes well beyond financial or real estate considerations. Moving after re-tirement requires careful consideration, especially if, as in Janice's case, one person wants to move and the other does not.

Rather than tell Les and Janice what they should do, I wanted to make them aware of a few housing considerations that contribute to re-tirement happiness.

I turned to Les and said, "You mentioned that you would like to move but it seems that this may present problems for Janice. Why do you want to move?"

"I think we would be better off if we move," said Les.

"Better off in what way?" I asked.

"Well, we can save money by moving to a smaller community and we both love the outdoors. We usually spend our summers camping and fishing and we both love to ski. I don't have a spot picked out yet. But I thought that if we moved to a small city near the mountains, we would have the best of both worlds. Besides, if we sold our house we would have more money to live off."

"Your reasoning sounds good," I said. "But the problem is, it doesn't seem to be in sync with Janice's plans. So let's take a look at Janice's concern and see if you can find a solution, or at least a compromise."

I asked them if they knew anyone who moved after re-tirement and who, after moving, realized it was a mistake.

"Well, yes," said Les. "This guy I used to work with and his wife moved back to England. They stayed about six months and didn't like it. I heard that they moved back."

"Like all issues in re-tirement," I said, "just because you know of one case where a plan did not work out, it does not necessarily follow that it will not work out for you. Having said that, we can learn a few things from your friend's experience, and certainly the decision to move should not be treated lightly."

I advised them to think about two very important questions. Firstly, can you satisfy your needs and skills in the new community? And next, if it doesn't work out, what are your alternatives? You don't want to be trapped there.

"Sometimes it's impossible to predict what it will be like living in a new community," I said, "until after the move. You have to expect the unexpected. You may miss old friends, the doctor and dentist who looked after you for years, your mechanic who you trust, your standing in the community, and familiar places filled with memories. And then again, retirement is a great opportunity for a new beginning."

My main concern was that they thought this through thoroughly, and reached a mutually agreed upon compromise. To start their thinking I told them about Sylvia who moved and encountered an unexpected problem. Here's what happened.

Sylvia was a widow. After she re-tired, she moved back to a small town where she came from to be near her family. She always enjoyed holidays back home, so now that she was free to live where she wanted, moving home seemed like a good idea. At first things went well but after a while she began to feel stifled by her family. They were always thinking about her and were concerned that she not be lonely. So, whenever her family members entertained they always included Sylvia. In return, when she entertained she felt obliged to invite her family.

But Sylvia wasn't lonely. She wanted to develop new friendships outside of her family sphere but constantly being with family kept her from developing new friendships. Because she was living in a small town she wasn't meeting anybody new. Her friendships were limited. She longed for the sense of independence that she used to feel. Unfortunately, she had sold her original home, housing prices began to rise, and she couldn't afford to buy another house in her former community. She eventually moved back, however, and continues to visit her family for special occasions only - as she used to do before she re-tired.

After I finished relating this story to Les and Janice, they looked a little pensive.

"I'm not trying to talk you out of moving," I said. "I'm just warning you to be cautious when moving because you never know what it will be like until you move there."

Don't Be Impulsive

To give them some guidelines, I said, "We can learn a few things from Sylvia's story. If you decide to move, the best piece of advice I can give you is, don't be too impulsive and don't burn your bridges. Don't buy a home before knowing that it is right for you. This can lead to grief."

I told them about Greg and Sara's experience. They lived in the Mid-West and took a holiday to visit their children who lived on the coast. After spending a week with the kids they took a side trip to a small town a few hours away. They came across a small house overlooking the ocean and Greg fell in love with it. According to Sara, Greg was all set to buy. This would be the re-tirement home of his dreams. She wasn't so sure, so she suggested that they wait until they had a chance to properly survey the area. They went back to spend a few more days with their children. Then they returned to the small town, checked into a motel, and after spending a few days there, they realized that this location was not right for them. Had they bought it impulsively, it would have been a big mistake. Fortunately Sara had the foresight to hold back on Greg's impulse.

"Buying impulsively can be disastrous," I said. "You never know what it will be like - or what you might miss - until you spend some time there."

I told them about a couple I met who moved from a big city to a small community. After a while, they began to miss their former neighbors. Although they used to live in a large city, they were part of a very tight community where they had very close ties. When they realized their mistake, they went back to their original neighborhood hoping to find a house to buy. They went door-to-door asking if anyone wanted to sell. Unfortunately, no one was willing. Eventually they bought a house four blocks away, but it was not the same. Being somewhat removed, they were not able to regain the tight friendships they had given up.

Satisfy Your Needs in the New Community

"Another important rule," I stressed, "is to ask yourself if you can satisfy your needs and skills in the new community. Can you find activities that are worthwhile and enjoyable? Of course you may never know until you move. But this important condition should be kept in mind."

"As I mentioned, we like to do things outdoors so I don't think this will be a problem for us," said Les.

"You never know," I replied. "Let me tell you about

somebody who encountered this problem after moving. His name is Stan and before he re-tired he and his wife used to spend the winters in a resort town in California. They thought that this would be the perfect place to re-tire. The weather was good, they both enjoyed playing golf, and over the years they had developed a small group of friends. So when Stan re-tired they sold their house and purchased a small house in this community. They spent some time fixing it up and about a year later they sold the house and bought a condominium. Six months later, they sold the condominium and bought another house.

"It became clear that their series of moves had nothing to do with housing per se. Stan was bored and kept busy by moving and fixing up the houses he bought. Sure he enjoyed golfing, and various other activities, but they didn't totally replace being at work. To compensate for this, he worked at moving. He didn't do this to make money; he was simply looking for something else to keep him busy. Eventually they moved back to their original home city, Stan became involved in a small business, and they have not moved since. They still visit California and thoroughly enjoy life."

Don't Burn Your Bridges

"Do you own your home?" I asked.

"Yes we do." said Janice.

"Then the next piece of advice I can offer is, if you move, 'don't burn your bridges'. Don't sell everything without giving your newly adopted home a trial run. If possible, rent out your present home and rent accommodations in the region where you plan to move. This may not compare to owning a home in the new community, but think of this as insurance.

After your trial period, you will then be able to judge what is best for you. If it doesn't work out, you still have your original house to move back to. If it works out, then make the move permanent by selling your house. Who knows, your house may be worth more after you rent it out for six months or a year. And by renting initially in the new community, you have flexibility after you learn more about where you want to live."

I went on to say, "Another piece of advice, which may not apply to you, is don't succumb to pressures from well meaning friends or even your children. You be the judge. Think about the lifestyle you want and the kind of people you are."

I told them about a couple I met who lived in a large house that was becoming a burden to both of them. They were spending too much time cleaning, and repairing things around the house. They had dreams of moving to a small farm. Unfortunately, their son did not want them to sell the house. He still lived at home and if his parents sold the house he would have nowhere to live. To avoid having to find and I suppose pay for his own place, he made his parents feel guilty for wanting to sell the family house.

"That really doesn't apply to us," said Les.

"I realize that," I replied, "I am telling you about a few situations I have come across because, as I mentioned before, you will never know what problems might come up after you move."

"OK," I said. "Let's take a look at the other slightly more thorny issue where Les wants to move but Janice doesn't."

I told them about Ann who said that her husband was an avid fisherman and hunter. When he re-tired, he wanted to move to a 40-acre property that was at least a 30-minute drive to civilization. Ann told us that she went with her husband to look at the property and she just sat in the car crying. She knew that if they moved there she would be bored out of her mind and would hate every minute of it. Clearly she had a dilemma.

As another example, I met a woman who told me that her husband wanted to move back to Bermuda, his birthplace. But she didn't want to move because she couldn't stand her in-laws.

It is not uncommon for one person to want to move back to where he or she came from and the other wants to stay where they are. Sometimes those people who think about moving back home forget why they left in the first place.

Situations where one person wants to move and the other doesn't may not have an easy solution. To minimize the potential problem, I emphasized to Les and Janice the need for compromise.

"Janice, if you decide to try a move and you haven't burned your bridges, do it with an open mind. If you expect to hate the new location, chances are it will become a self-fulfilling prophecy. It will come true. This means that both of you should work towards finding worthwhile and enjoyable pursuits in the new community. If you are both able to satisfy your needs and skills in the new community, then in all probability the move will turn into a positive experience. If not, and if you are not trapped, you can always move back to where you came from, or to another location."

People who think about moving after re-tirement may never get this thought out of their system until they try it. So, by all means go for it. Having said that, you must be prepared to expect the unexpected, and not put yourself in a position where you are not able to either come back to where you came from, or move on to somewhere else. If it doesn't work out and if you are able to rectify the situation, you will have gained from the experience. You have learned that your original thought of moving was not for you.

"Well," I asked, "has that helped your situation?"

"Yes it has," said Les. "I still really want to move and I know that it might be a problem for Janice. But, and I think you will agree with me on this Janice, we both have some things to think about. The most important thing I have learned is that we shouldn't sell our house until we are sure about this move."

"And what are your thoughts on this, Janice?" I asked.

"I was thinking the same thing as Les. I guess I would be more willing to try it knowing that we had something to come back to."

I encouraged Les and Janice to continue talking and thinking about what we had discussed. I assured them again that many couples have faced similar problems and that they were not insurmountable. They thanked me and left feeling, I believe, optimistic about the future.

Chapter Summary

- Before considering a move ask yourself two important questions: Can I (we) satisfy my needs and skills in the new location? And, if it doesn't work out, what are the alternatives? You do not want to be trapped there.

- Don't be impulsive. You will never know what it will be like or what you might miss until you spend some time in the new community.

- Don't burn your bridges. Don't sell your home or purchase a home in the new community until you are sure that the new community is right for you. Then when you are sure, make the move permanent by selling your home and buying in the new community.

- If one partner is reluctant to move but willing to try, do so with an open mind. If you expect the worst, chances are it will become a self-fulfilling prophecy.

Retired Teachers

Twenty seven percent moved at or following retirement. Their reasons included:

Reason	Percent
To get a home of more appropriate size	28%
To be nearer family or friends	26%
To live in a nicer area	25%
Reduce home maintenance responsibilities	25%
A better climate	24%
Reduce cost of housing	11%
Moved to a retirement community	6%

Other reasons:

Needed more room for horse operation
Built new house in desired location
Moved to the farm which I grew up on and inherited.
Home destroyed by fire
A home to take in a parent
Moved to a metropolitan area for health care, arts etc
Husband's job
Dislike of neighborhood
One floor living
Located close to a community with cultural activities

(Continued)

Distance of Move

Less than 10 miles/km	26%
10-20 miles/km	10%
21-100 miles/km	23%
More than 100 miles/km	43%

Advice On Moving

People who had moved were asked if they had any advice or recommendations for people who are thinking about moving at or following retirement. Although the advice varied from very specific to general, three distinct categories emerged.

1) Think about what you are giving up or leaving behind

"Stay close to family and friends. Do not move so far away that seeing them becomes a hardship."

"Think long and hard before you leave your support base."

"Take into consideration the value of established friendships, of your reputation in your community."

"Visit the area several times to be certain that the area has all the requirements you are looking for. I know many people who have moved and been very unhappy because they were no longer near friends/family."

(Continued)

2) Don't be hasty

Think carefully about re-locating. Don't make spur-of-the-moment decisions.

Do not do it right away. The burden of moving away from friends and family adds another unnecessary stress on the changes of retirement."

"Don't make decisions too quickly—settle in the "retirement routine" first."

"Spend time looking for new home; Select a location and home you like (with minimum upkeep) as opposed to relocating near your children."

3) Try it first

"First of all, figure out all of your needs, present and future, and see if a move would fill those needs. Think of WHY you would move. Is it a good reason? Perhaps a long vacation to where you are considering moving would be a good idea, just to try it out. Would you be able to pull up stakes and fit into a new community easily?"

"Take time staying in the new area prior to buying a place. Ask others who live in that new area how they like the area."

"Investigate the area. Rent a house or condo for a year before deciding to move. It is too expensive to move out of a place you misjudged."

(Continued)

"Before you move, spend some time at the new location to make sure this is what you want to do - the more time, the better."

"If you are not moving back to the area in which you grew up, take a week for each area you think you are interested in. Get info about each of these places before you visit. Audition your choices."

Practical advice for moving into a new community

"Think of your needs in the next 10 to 20 years and that will help you determine if this is going to be a good move for you. Try to find an area that is just developing — the prices are less expensive. Stay away from overcrowded communities that have traffic problems and require too much travel to get to the places you need, like shopping, doctors, restaurants, etc. Consider the cost of living for the area and also the CLIMATE— thousands of people move out of Florida and other hot climates within a year of moving to those areas. Consider moving closer to family or friends that can help you in time of need – it's no fun being on your own when you need assistance due to health problems, etc."

"Don't sit down and expect opportunities to come to you. You need to seek out activities to be involved in. They are out there, but you need to knock on some doors."

(Continued)

"Consider what you will do with your time to stay busy but feel important."

"My wife and I were familiar with the area where we were moving. We knew people here, and were comfortable with the idea of moving here. That helped a great deal."

"Think of lifestyle after retirement and search for best location to fit. We've moved twice since retirement because my husband didn't seriously investigate the potential for pursuing his hobbies."

"Do the homework: ask about monthly expenses such as electricity, gas, phone, water, etc. Find out about taxes; Shop around for realtors, brokers, etc."

"Before you move investigate both quality and ACCESSIBILITY of health care, dentistry, car services (mechanic and general services), repair and maintenance on residence, and driving distances to shop and traffic patterns to deal with. With gasoline at $2.70/gallon, it is more than an irritation to sit in a traffic jam. Also, think emotionally about who and WHAT you're leaving behind: a special restaurant with many memories; the stores where people know you; friends and neighbors; church, temple, or mosque; even the political climate (for those so inclined). I think many people think excitedly about NEW places, friends, etc., but 'letting go' is not the same for a 65 - 70 year old as it is for a 20 - 25 year old - neither physically nor psychologically."

(Continued)

"We moved to get to a ranch house, everything on one floor. Consider what you can do to your present house so that you can live on one floor if necessary. That would have saved us money."

"I would wait a year or two to adjust to retirement, since moving and retirement are two major lifestyle changes."

"I spent many hours researching to find what we wanted. The Internet was my prime source of that research. We also did some traveling to access different communities."

Lesson Learned:

If you are thinking about moving, a) think about what you are giving up or leaving behind, b) don't be hasty, and c) try it first. Even if you are familiar with the area, you will never know what it will be like until you spend some time at the new location. As one person put it, "*audition your choices*".

11

Go Where You Wanna Go

(*Mamas & Papas, 1966*)

The Retired Teachers Survey included three open-ended or qualitative questions focusing on, a) the main attractions of re-tirement, b) the drawbacks, and, c) advice for teachers who are about to re-tire. This section of the survey gave your re-tirement mentors the opportunity to freely express and elaborate on their opinions, impressions and experiences before and after re-tirement. The responses to each question ranged widely – as one would expect – but they present an excellent perspective on re-tirement from those teachers who 'have been there'. As you read through the impressions and advice of your re-tired colleagues, you will see contradictions and

---

NOTE: To give structure or order to the 1,200 responses, each response was evaluated and in the process we identified general categories based on the type of response. This process enabled us to determine percentages of respondents in each category. Due to the opportunity for multiple responses, totals may exceed 100%. Also, I used re-tire (with a dash) throughout my comments, and retire (without the dash) in the verbatim text of the survey respondents.

repetition. One would expect this as we are looking at re-tirement from 400 different perspectives. This of course is the nature of all life experiences and re-tirement is no exception. Hopefully after surveying the comments by your re-tired colleagues, you will learn more about what you can expect from and how to plan for your re-tirement.

The Main Attractions of Re-tirement

The main attractions of re-tirement can broadly be classified into responses that reflect the 'Push' and 'Pull' factors introduced in Chapter 6 (The Decision to Re-tire). As a reminder, the push factors included those that in a sense are pushing the individual into re-tirement (the things that you may be happy to give up), and the pull factors include the benefits of re-tirement (the things you look forward to in re-tirement).

The main attractions of re-tirement include:

Freedom/More time for myself	91%
No deadlines, stress or work responsibilities	21%

A) Freedom/More Time For Myself

Clearly the main overriding benefit of re-tirement is the freedom it brings. You will:

- Have more time for yourself
- Be able to please yourself
- Set your own pace
- Do things you have always wanted to do but never had time for while you are working

- No longer be at the mercy of the clock or calendar
- Be busy by choice doing what you choose to be busy at
- Be in control of your own time
- Be your own boss

Freedom is the 'pull' factor and the implication here is having the opportunity to do as you choose, which often stands in direct contrast to work. For example, some of your re-tired colleagues had the following thoughts:

Time is mainly your own. No bells control your comings and goings unless you want them to. Time to smell the roses and try new hobbies.

Challenge of doing different things because you want to do them. Time to do things that you did not have time to do while working full time.

I now have the time to do what I want on MY schedule. I can travel at non-peak times and stay that extra day or two if I wish. I can take off for the weekend knowing I don't have to spend Sunday evening writing lesson plans or checking papers. *I can now engage in volunteer and hobby activities that time would not have permitted when I was teaching.*

Freedom to do what I want; when I want. While teaching was the love of my life, it limited my travel and plans to set times. Oh, I realize that those summers off were the envy of non-teachers, but what they didn't understand was the inability to take a couple of weeks in my preference.

The freedom to plan each day's activities around my own interests...a freedom never experienced before; and the time to be involved in organizations and causes about which I am passionate. Time to spend with family is a top attraction. I may be poorer financially, but I am my own boss.

Freedom to do the things I didn't have time for without guilt. Having time to take part in more social things. Time to learn about things purely for personal reasons with no practical goal in sight.

A varied daily schedule; ability to do those things that I'd postponed until I had the free time to do them; freedom from the daily preparations; freedom from correcting papers; freedom to travel; freedom from attempting to resolve the behavior problems of students; get up and go when you're ready - no need to punch a time clock.

B) No Deadlines, Stress or Work Responsibilities

Another attraction of re-tirement is the relief it can bring from the stress and pressures of teaching. These are the 'push' factors. According to your re-tirement mentors, life in re-tirement can be more peaceful and relaxing, less stressful, and you can please yourself without feeling guilty.

Life is more peaceful without hectic schedules and work hassles. It would have been nice to have kept a scrapbook of the thirty-one years. I never thought I'd be teaching for so long.

Lack of stress and pressure, greater flexibility, opportunity to do nothing without feeling too guilty

The choices! Not having to keep a schedule. Being rested and not fatigued/stressed all the time. Being able to spend time with family as I wish or they need. Having freedom to pursue activities which had been 'on hold' for many years. Relief from mental stress. Time to spend just for me. I think it all boils down to having enough TIME FOR LIVING!

Less stress, less paperwork, less trying to fulfill things that have nothing to do with the teaching process.

More time with my family, less stress!! More time to relax, did I mention less stress?

Relaxation: less stress which was a health benefit to me: more time to do what I want to do: Got away from a working situation which was less than healthy

I taught in very stressful conditions so freedom from those pressures is the main attraction. Also, having the time to do whatever interests me.

Less stress and lower blood pressure; opportunity to meet more interesting people and, perhaps best of all, time to finally smell the roses (or homemade cinnamon buns).

The Main Drawbacks of Re-tirement

To balance the equation, your re-tirement mentors were asked to list the main drawbacks of re-tirement. Replies to this question fell into three broad categories – financial concerns, social loses including contact with friends, colleagues and students, and problems encountered in re-tirement. It is important to note, however, that not everyone had problems, and in some cased the problems were minimal. Also, when asked how satisfied they were with re-tirement, 69% were very satisfied and 29% were reasonably satisfied.

The main drawbacks of retirement that were identified include:

Financial Concerns	43%
Social Losses	32%
Psychological Losses	24%
There are no drawbacks	15%
Other	10%

A) Financial Concerns

Financial concerns in re-tirement reflect (in part) differences in the respondents' pension plan and healthcare benefits. Your re-tirement mentors included both American and Canadians and the latter have the benefit of universal health care. Because your income (from teaching) will be reduced you will have to learn how to budget your money. But as several people mentioned, your expenses will also be reduced.

The main drawback is not being as financially free as all of the ads on television would have you believe! And you have to be really careful when traveling with health concerns.

The main drawback is not enough money. Everything is going up but our income.

You need to learn to live on less income, but you save on such items as a school wardrobe, teaching related materials and supplies, union dues, daily lunch away from home, plus other expenses. You might miss the process of teaching, but you can sub teach to fulfill that need.

The biggest shock was turning 65 and finding our finances were in jeopardy. Everything was so much more; health plans were now very expensive. We were lucky just when we thought we were going to have deep problems we inherited some money that saved us.

Not enough money, skyrocketing healthcare costs putting a dent in my pocketbook. Otherwise I am as happy as I have ever been.

Not having the same amount of money coming in each month...while at the same time, having more time to spend money.

Less money, less money, less money—but, hey, money isn't everything!

Another drawback is being paid once a month. You really have to budget your money well. And be sure to save money on a regular basis.

B) Social Losses

According to your re-tirement mentors, next to a reduced income, giving up contact with colleagues and the students and being part of the team is another important drawback of re-tirement. As we saw earlier, Mixing with people was the most frequently mentioned reason for working in re-tirement (66%), and the most frequently mentioned loss from teaching (37%).

Probably the biggest drawback has been that I miss many of my friends and colleagues who are still working. Chatting with them once in a while on the phone or an occasional lunch just isn't the same as seeing them on the daily basis.

I miss the children. I miss their enthusiasm, their energy, their spirit, their creativity and their hugs!! Good thing that I now have three grandchildren to compensate.

Reduced social interactions with other members of the faculty; no longer being part of a team.

Missing the interaction with other teachers and the satisfaction of making a difference in a child's life.

I really do miss the interaction with my students. I miss those wonderful "aha" moments when the "dawn" of learning breaks. I miss reading the creative, well-written compositions, poems, stories, of my students, and sharing the pride when they won literary contests. I miss the joy of reading aloud from books the students loved. I miss the love and respect from my students and my opportunities to show them how much I love, appreciate, and respect them. I miss watching them grow intellectually and watching them mature in so many ways. I miss the feelings of accomplishment that are so exhilarating and "heady"! I miss the interaction with my co-workers, my principal, the staff, and support personnel. I miss the excitement of starting fresh in the fall with new faces, new minds, new challenges, and new experiences of learning and getting to know one another.

I am a "people person" so I really miss the interaction with my friends and peers every day.

C) Psychological Losses

Psychological losses include feeling of boredom, lack of intellectual stimulation, lack of daily structure or routine, reduced motivation, lack of identity, purpose, and so on. This was only mentioned by 24% of respondents, but it is something to look out for.

If I could go back to the months before I retired, I would try to work time management skills. I was not prepared for the challenge this has become. I am struggling to get exercise, and healthful habits into my day just as much as I was when I was teaching. I never dreamed this would be a problem. I retired with little preparation. It is working OK and the problems I'm having are within my power to solve.

The hardest part for me is letting go of the structure and accountability that I had while teaching. Letting myself really relax has been hard.

Boredom, had to volunteer to keep busy, too much free time... don't like to read or watch T.V.

It is easy to become "lazy" about structuring your day when it seems you have all the time in the world to get things done. I find it is important to maintain a quasi- schedule.

Possibility of being bored if not engaged in activities or a routine. Not feeling productive if you do not involve yourself with meaningful directions.

I miss being "the teacher". I lost some of my identity when I retired.

Lack of purpose in daily routine; consequently I experience a minimal sense of satisfaction in daily accomplishments.

Losing the feeling that I was contributing to society in a very important way.

The psychological change of going from full time work and responsibility to not having to work and being out of the work environment is very real and must be dealt with. I also used to be on the "cutting edge" of technology and enjoyed teaching it to other teachers as well as the students. I do miss that aspect of my job.

Advice From Your Re-tired Colleagues

The third open-ended question gave your re-tirement mentors the opportunity to provide advice for teachers who are approaching re-tirement. This resulted in five main types of responses. The two most common responses focused on the importance of planning – both your time and your finances. Others interpreted the question by referring to making the decision to re-tire, and some mentioned the benefits of volunteering as detailed below;

Plan Your Time	44%
Plan Your Finances	33%
Consideration when deciding to re-tire	31%
Benefits of Volunteering	11%
Other	16%

A) Plan Your Time

Based on our extensive Life Goal Planning workshop experience for thousands of pre-re-tirees, only about one-third has concrete future plans before they re-tire. The central focus of this book is to help you replace satisfactions lost from teaching as a key to your re-tirement happiness. So, it is no surprise that the most frequently mentioned advise by your re-tirement mentors was to develop a plan with respect to how you will spend your time in re-tirement. Part 2 of this book, includes the tools to plan your time in re-tirement.

Make certain you have interests that will keep you busy, keep your mind and body occupied. Volunteer, develop a hobby if you don't already have one, get out and be around people if you don't have family and friends around you. You aren't your job. There is life in retirement. I have a friend who retired last year and who had no idea what she was going to do. She planned to go back to teaching part-time, but our system is in financial trouble and RIF'd a lot of staff...no chance for her to be employed. She's taking the oil painting classes she never had the time for before, she's delivering Meals on Wheels, and this summer she's participating in a Sister City project, going to China for five weeks, three weeks of which will be spent teaching English and American culture to Chinese high school students. There are so many things to do that teachers simply don't have the time for if they're doing a good job teaching. Now that you're retired, do them!

I think it is important to start looking at retirement before the time comes and a person is ready. That gives a person time to prepare for retirement in many different ways. I started looking at retirement 6 years before I retired. I was able to prepare myself and think about what I wanted to do after retirement. It gave me time to look around. I am a happily retired teacher.

If you are doing something you love, also have plans of what to do with your time. One can only do so much fishing, traveling, eating out, etc. The feel of accomplishment may be missing. Plan, plan, plan!

Be sure you are certain about what you want and/or expect from retirement. I know some colleagues who didn't know what to do with themselves because they had cultivated no other interests during the years they were employed. They were left somewhat floundering.

Plan carefully to have "something to do" each day so that one doesn't have time on their hands and wonder what to do with it. Staying active is the best way to stay "young".

Plan how you are going to fashion your new life. What interests will you pursue? How will you restructure your social life, your leisure time? Don't rush into anything. Think it through. Expect to find your focus changing as you mature. Project what you want to see or be in 5 years, in 10 years, in 20 years. Expect to feel a little lost and unsure of yourself. It takes at least a year, and often two, to settle in to the new lifestyle. No school opening in September takes getting used to!

Become psychologically prepared. Know yourself and what you need to have and do in order to live a satisfying life on your terms. Take workshops, Do extensive reading and have peer discussions on topics like coping with change, redefining yourself in terms of skills and how they can be "recycled" in retirement. Also, survey your community to see where the needs or gaps in service are and then match them to your interests and skills. Another area may be turning a hobby into a business or, at least to create pocket money for fun or to donate to your favorite charity. I find some of my retired friends don't realize the wide variety of skills they possess. If one wants to work, one has just to make it known because others often recognize your skills even if you don't. The possibilities for activity, whether it be volunteer or work for pay are endless.

B) Plan Your Finances

If you haven't already done so, in addition to planning your time, your re-tirement mentors strongly encourage you to plan your finances – the earlier the better.

Start saving money when you start teaching, even if it is a small amount every payday. Retirement is even more fantastic if you have lots of money. However, even if you don't have lots of money, you can enjoy retirement. Go to every pre-retirement seminar that you can attend.

The only thing I think I could have done better would be to have saved more money! I think we should be fine, however the more one saves, the more peace of mind I think one would have.

Early in your career consult a financial planner and begin a savings program then - do not wait!

Money does become a factor as I age as expenses are always increasing - real estate taxes, utilities, fuel, groceries. There is no increase in the amount of funds coming in which makes budgeting difficult. Still we are comfortable and do most of the things we wish to do but we must turn to our savings for extras. Of course we saved for our retirement so here we are.

You must begin your tax sheltered and savings program when you begin your work. You owe it to yourself, if only a few dollars to begin. The only things I would change about my professional and personal career is that I would begin saving earlier.

Be sure you have investments to fill in the gap. My retirement check was plenty when I first retired, but with cost of living, it isn't as much as I need now.

Take advantage of retirement planning being offered. Retirement is wonderful when you feel financially secure. Your expense structure changes so it is helpful to talk to people who have been retired for some time to benefit from their experiences. For example- Our dry cleaning bills decreased as our wardrobes became more casual, but gas usage increased since we are driving more now. Our food budget shifted in some areas. We are spending more time traveling but can take advantage of off-peak prices. It is a good idea to make a chart of expected changes to avoid surprises.

C) The Decision Process

When asked their advice, some of your re-tirement mentors included the process they went through or their reasons for making the decision to re-tire when they did. Several people gave the response that I refer to as the 'Nike' approach - "Just do it!"

I had promised myself that when my years were over I was going to walk out and that no one would have to ask me to leave. That is the way I did it.

In general, however, I would not recommend that anyone retire as suddenly as I did. More preparation, even one workshop that covered the Non-financial issues would have been useful.

Consider retirement if you feel that the teaching job has taken on more of a bookkeeping role, rather than a teaching role. Then pursue other activities that make you happy.

Don't work until you burn yourself out and can't physically or mentally enjoy retirement. The education business gets tougher each year and I see many more burned out educators that left very little or nothing of themselves for retirement. You only live once and you might as well enjoy it before the ride is over!!

Do it whenever you feel like you don't have the energy to keep teaching—don't wait to get to a certain number of years. I felt like I was slowing down—everything took longer to do—I felt myself losing patience with things that didn't bother me before. I wanted to retire while people still wanted me to keep teaching, not wait until they started thinking I should go.

If you can imagine yourself not returning to school, go for it while you are still young enough to enjoy it.

Retire!!!!!!!!! There are other activities that you can do which make you feel as productive as you were as a teacher. There are many activities that can take you beyond the classroom. It is possible to find a new path to success.

Be very sure in your mind that it is the time for YOU. Do not keep on if teaching isn't kind to you but if you still love what you are doing don't let anyone guilt you into retiring before YOU are READY!

If you are under a great deal of stress and feel that you are in a situation that is not favorable, then think very hard about retiring. Make sure that you are able to continue your lifestyle in retirement.

E) Benefits of Volunteering

When asked their advice about retiring some respondents mentioned the benefits of volunteering. In a sense this response is a sub-set of the advice to 'plan your time' because volunteering in re-tirement is generally viewed as a replacement for work. In addition to praising the benefits of volunteering, several people offered cautions – things to look out for.

Volunteer work is very rewarding and also you feel appreciated- something sometimes not seen in the workplace.

If you aren't interested in volunteering in schools or returning to part-time teaching - join a local chapter of Retired Teachers - they're great people and will become new friends. Volunteer activities are a great way to give back to the community - be it Hospice, church, or even political. A big page in your book of life will be turned and what you script will be entirely up to you. Go for it!!

There are ample opportunities out there to help someone. You can tutor students after school or within the school day. You can drive for Meals on Wheels. You can work in hospitals and retirement centers/nursing homes. My wife and I work for an RV organization called NOMADS. The organization is similar to Habitat for Humanity in that we build or recondition homes and churches for the poor and needy. Working 6 hours a day four days a week, we have met the most wonderful people you could imagine in such colorful settings as Selma, AL, Homestead, FL, El Paso, TX, Tucson, AZ and many other places. There are countless opportunities for such volunteering. Pick as many as you feel you can do WELL.

In addition to the benefits of volunteering, several people mentioned the problem of others taking advantage of their free time, or advice on how to approach volunteering.

You can become too regimented if you accept every plea for you to volunteer. Relax and feel the waters before becoming too involved; after all you're life was not your own when teaching full time.

Learn that it IS okay to say NO to groups who want you to volunteer your time. You could be busy every day all day if you say yes to every organization who calls begging for volunteers. Choose the one/ones YOU are most interested in supporting and don't feel guilty about saying NO

People think since you are retired that you don't have anything to do. I am asked constantly asked to volunteer for this or that. I am confident enough to say no if I don't want to do it.

D) Other Advice

Friends and relatives take advantage of you, as they seem to be of the opinion, "well, now that you have nothing to do, could you do for me". Elderly parents think you are theirs full time and siblings tend to let the one who is retired carry the burden of their care.

Get over defining a good day by what work you accomplished. Be ready to accept yourself worthy of days when you accomplished lots of relaxation! If you are a workaholic, beware...it will be a rough adjustment.

Place emphasis on retiring to something rather than retiring from something.

If you have 25 years in education, please retire, enjoy life, and let a younger teacher have your position.

Leave as soon as possible. The stress is not worth it. My health has improved since retirement. It's great!

On the whole, your health will become better as the stress of work is taken away. One may find if they go back to teaching for short periods after retirement that it is more enjoyable because it was your choice to go that day. I find that my spouse and I have gotten closer because now we have time to share with each other.

You will no longer be following a set daily routine, so get a pocket calendar to keep track of your new activities. Finally, take a trip in September; the world outside the classroom is amazing (and a whole lot less crowded) at that time of year.

Don't think all will be rosy. Your circumstances may change, but life will still be challenging. You will miss out on some thing but you will have new experiences to pursue. Please don't sit back and vegetate, life is what you make it and you can make it dead, or you can make it your dream.

Do your travel immediately as health will determine if and when you will travel. Join organizations and activities with like-minded retirees. Stay away from your old work place—it will make you feel very old. Join the Y or structure your walking. Exercising helps you meet fellow retirees as well as making you feel good about yourself. Turn off the TV during the morning and afternoon—unless there is something very, very special. Watch out for the weekday second cocktail. Make a list of your goals, then objectives and cross them off as you do them. Structure your leisure reading— do an author study. Start writing your story as well as favored possessions.

Discuss the possibilities with your spouse - do you plan to stay home? Do you plan to work? If work, part-time or full time? Do you want to audit college courses or enroll to further your education? Will you become an automatic babysitting service for family if you stay at home? Can you make it on your retirement should something happen to your spouse?

Don't measure what you have accomplished each day. Learn to take time and enjoy the activities that you engage in, and that engage you. Follow your fancies and explore the areas that you didn't have time for before.

Do not wrap your personal identity so closely into your role of teacher so that you forget how to be wife/husband or parent. Look at retirement as the beginning or another life...one in which you can decide what comes next...the sky's the limit! One additional thing: try to stay healthy so that all possibilities are still within your reach and you are not limited by some physical or mental infirmity.

I think that a program of sabbaticals, which gave people some time away and then, extended their working years might be helpful.

Be prepared to make a transition from a busy life to a quieter life. Some friends who still work may resent your freedom from work. If you don't work afterwards, be prepared for the repeated question "What do you do all day?" Tell yourself that you earned your retirement!

12

Imagine
(*John Lennon, 1971*)

I have now shared with you the theory behind Life Goal Planning and the Road Map to Re-tirement Happiness. You learned that the secret to re-tirement happiness is to replace satisfactions lost from work and in Chapter 3 we had a brief look at a workshop that will enable you to identify your needs and skills, evaluate future plans, and come up with new plans. As a bonus, you have the benefit of learning from the experiences, impressions and advice of 400 re-tired teachers – your re-tirement mentors.

Understanding the theory behind a worthwhile and enjoyable re-tirement is only the first step however. To truly benefit, you have to put theory into practice. I now encourage you to complete the workshop on your own or with a small group as presented in Part 2. Remember, these exercises are valuable at any time during your pre re-tirement planning or after re-tirement.

Before turning to Part 2, you might be interested to learn how Dave and Diane, Les and Janice and Lynn's re-tirement careers unfolded.

Dave's Re-tirement Career

In Dave's words, "As you know, I struggled a bit trying to decide when to re-tire. Well, much to my surprise they came out with an early re-tirement incentive offer that I just couldn't resist - so I took the plunge. I really didn't know what to do with myself but my son-in-law, Eric, offered me a sales job so I thought, what the heck, why not give it a try.

"I was a bit wary because it can present extra problems working for family. Don't get me wrong, I like my son-in-law, but after teaching for over 35 years, I was concerned about how I would feel working for Eric. If we had problems working together I didn't want them to spill over into our personal life. We discussed this and agreed that we wouldn't let problems at work affect our personal life. But you never know.

"To make a long story short, after discussing it with Diane, I decided to join Eric. I was pretty much my own boss and I set my own hours. This was a definite plus for me. I was working part-time but I am the type of guy who likes to keep busy and gives 100% to the job, so I was putting in quite a bit of time and energy. I didn't mind because I was developing sales brochures and order forms and at first it was working out fairly well. We didn't do a lot of business but I enjoyed it and met some very nice people. It got me out of the house, and in the beginning it was a challenge.

"This went on for about five months. I really didn't need the extra money, and I started to feel that there must be something else I could do that would be more, shall we say, satisfying. I enjoyed it in the beginning at the developmental stage, but it started to get boring. Besides, I really didn't feel 100% comfortable having my son-in-law as a boss. But I didn't know what else I could do.

"Diane reminded me that re-tirement was a career and that I should look upon working with Eric as the first step. She encouraged me to look back at the Needs and Skills List I developed when we got together with Les and Janice. To be honest with you, I didn't give it a lot of thought when I retired because when the early re-tirement offer came through, I grabbed it and at the time it looked as though joining Eric would be a good idea. But when I decided to quit working for Eric things were different.

"I didn't have any other options so I went back to my Needs and Skills List and went through the questions again to make it more complete. I did this on my own. Then I asked myself if any of the needs or skills on my list were not satisfied. It was a worthwhile and interesting exercise because when I took a close look at my list the thing that stood out was I wanted to help others or give something back to society. Much to my surprise, when I looked at the suggestions that were made for me, and that I made for others during the brainstorming session, lo and behold, I made several suggestions that involved volunteering.

"So I looked into volunteering. I talked to several agencies and discovered that there is more to volunteering than I originally thought and I found many worthwhile causes. I felt a little guilty but to tell you the truth, I am not a volunteering kind of guy and nothing really appealed to me. So I was back to square one.

"A week later I was having a coffee and I ran into Pat, a teacher friend. He taught a computer course and asked me what I was doing. I told him about my dilemma. He told me something that I found very interesting. It seems that many of the kids in his computer class were mainly interested in playing computer games. The reason is, his school is in a less affluent area and some of the kids did not have computers at home. A one-class-a-week computer course was not seen as important. They just wanted to play games.

"As we talked I recalled a friend who told me that the company he worked for upgraded all of their computers. In the process they got rid of several old computers. Some staff members bought computers, but many computers were thrown out. It's not as though they were broken; they were perfectly good computers. It seems that they were old technology and weren't worth anything. Pat said that was a shame. He knew plenty of kids who could use them at home for their school-work and he assured me that they were not obsolete for that purpose. It seemed to me that if his company upgraded and threw out computers, there must be many others doing the same.

"Suddenly, like a bolt of lightning from the sky, my future began to unfold. I thought, why not start up a sort of clearing house to supply discarded computers to kids who needed them? I got very excited about this idea and Pat and I started to throw around several ideas. He got so enthusiastic that he volunteered to help in his spare time. I laughed at this suggestion. A few days ago I felt guilty because I couldn't find a volunteer agency that appealed to me, and today Pat is volunteering to help me.

"Since our first meeting things started to move quickly. The original idea was to help needy kids get computers. But in talking to various people, I discovered a program in another city that we modeled our program after. Why reinvent the wheel? We received a small government grant and set up a non-profit organization called Computers for Kids. We use donated space in a community center and run classes teaching kids basic computer skills. Pat talked to several teachers who volunteered to teach the course in their spare time. Meanwhile, I am scouring the city and a few of my friends from work are helping me find computers. The best part is, after the students complete the course, they are given a computer to use at home. It's a great concept. The kids learn computer basics and as an incentive, those who complete the course receive a free computer. I love being involved in it.

"Oh yes, I forget to mention. Diane is helping with Computers For Kids. She looks after the office work, and loves it. In fact, she is thinking of taking some office management and accounting courses. Her only regret is that she didn't do something like this years ago.

"When I think back, I have to admit that when I re-tired the idea of helping kids with computers never occurred to me. In fact, if somebody had suggested it to me, I probably would have thought they were nuts. But it's amazing how one thing leads to another and eventually I found the perfect thing for me. If I had not started with Eric, I would never have met Pat and would not have come up with the idea of Computers For Kids. I'm not making any money from this, but that doesn't matter. I get a lot of satisfaction from what I am doing and it leaves me plenty of time to pursue other things like camping, my workshop, and spending time with Diane. It took me about a year to reach this point in my re-tirement career. And who knows what the future holds. But for now, I couldn't be happier."

Les's Re-tirement Career

In Les's words, "I admit that when I first re-tired I was having some problems. I felt that the solution was to move to a new life in a small town where we could be close to a lot of outdoor activities. Janice was not too keen on the idea. She enjoys outdoor activities but was concerned about leaving behind our friends, daughter and grandchildren. After a great deal of thought and discussion, Janice agreed to try it. In case things did not work out, we didn't sell our house. We rented it to my wife's niece and a few of her friends. They needed a place to live for the school year and that worked out just right for us.

"Over the years we used to ski with our kids and often rented a chalet at the same ski area. The chalet was at the foot of the mountain. This was especially convenient when the kids were younger. They could walk into the village and meet their friends. So when Janice and I moved, we went back to the same area. It held a lot of good memories for us and we rented a small chalet near the main ski village. It was quite expensive but we thought it would be best to be as close to the facilities as possible.

"It didn't take us long to discover that it wasn't necessary for Janice and I to live at the foot of the mountain. First of all, it was expensive. Also it's different when you live there year round. We found that it was too busy, especially on weekends, so we started to look for an alternative. We visited a small town about 10 miles away and our first impression was very favorable. It was an older and smaller village but because it was a few miles away from the main ski village, real estate was significantly cheaper. There were several new condominium developments in this village and we spent some time looking around and talking to different people. We went back and forth trying to decide what to do. This village was not part of our original plans, yet it did have some appeal. Although we felt uncertain about making another move, it helped knowing that we still owned our house in the city. We felt secure that if this didn't work out, we wouldn't be homeless. It was like experimenting with a new lifestyle knowing that our old lifestyle was waiting in the wings if we wanted it back.

"We found a unit that we liked and rented it on a month-to-month basis with the option to purchase. This way we could try it out for a while, and then decide if we wanted to make it permanent. Soon after we moved in we started to meet people who were also re-tired. Eventually, we decided to buy the condo and we are both delighted with our new home. When the school year is up we plan to sell our house in the city. As an added bonus, according to the real estate agent, our house will probably be worth more when we sell it compared to what it was worth when we first rented it out.

"All in all, things have worked out pretty well for us. Our cost of living is lower where we are now. When we sell our house in the city, we can pay off our condominium and put something aside for a rainy day. We have met several great couples and Janice and I have spent plenty of time together hiking and enjoying the outdoors. When winter comes, we are really looking forward to ski season. We have extra room for when our children come to visit. This way we can see our grandchildren but our children are not calling all the time for us to baby-sit. All in all, things have worked out very well."

Lynn's Re-tirement Career

In Lynn's words, "I haven't actually re-tired yet. I took a look at my needs and skills met through work and decided that most were being met. There was no reason for me to re-tire. Actually, that realization was a load off my mind.

"Also, by looking at my needs and skills at work, I realized that there were some areas where I could make some changes. For instance, I became more involved in our student-training program. I am enjoying my interaction with the students. I find it to be very challenging and stimulating - something that was missing from my work.

"I am starting to think about re-tirement, although it is a few years off. One thing I am thinking about doing is going into teaching, maybe to teach law. If I can't do that, I will think about other ways to get involved in teaching because I totally enjoy my interaction with the students. Ironically, thinking about re-tirement has helped to improve my work. But I guess I am lucky. I don't have to re-tire until I am ready.

"If I had to summarize what I learned from Life Goal Planning, I would say that if I had a million dollars in the bank, which I don't, I would still wait until I am ready to re-tire. I will be ready to re-tire when I can satisfy more of my needs outside of rather than inside work."

Concluding Comments

You now have the theory behind re-tirement happiness and have learned how to create worthwhile and enjoyable re-tirement activities. All that remains is to put this theory and knowledge into practice. This book does not end until you reach your destination and find activities in re-tirement that you consider worthwhile and enjoyable. So refer to it whenever you need some inspiration or a refresher. Enjoy the journey!

Chapter Summary

- They all lived happily ever after.

Part 2

Life Goal Planning Workshop Instructions

This workshop is your key to re-tirement happiness; it will assist you to replace satisfaction lost from work. Actively completing all of the exercises may change your life. You can benefit from this workshop at any time - before or after you re-tire.

The workshop can be completed individually, but for best results I highly recommend a small group of friends/ relatives who are interested in planning the non-financial aspects of their re-tirement. It is highly recommended that your group include spouses.

Ideally everyone in the group will read this book in advance to learn the basics of Life Goal Planning, however, this is not necessary. Simply designate a group facilitator to read the following instructions aloud. The instructions are presented as a verbatim script progressing through the various workshop stages. The facilitator should allow enough time to complete each exercise. In some cases there will be an obvious pause, and I have highlighted the word {Pause} in brackets as appropriate. Should you choose to split the workshop into two sessions, a natural break could occur following Stage 3.

Materials - Each person requires several sheets of lined paper and a pen or pencil. Write the following headings on separate sheets of paper.

- Re-tirement Plans
- Suggestions Received
- Suggestions Given
- Brainstorming Notes
- Activity Evaluation List – on this sheet create 4 columns. The column on the left should be about 4 inches wide and it is headed "Needs & Skills". The next 3 columns should be about 1 inch each and they are headed with the numbers '1', '2', '3'. You may wish to have available additional copies of the Activity Evaluation List.

Activity Evaluation List

Needs & Skills	1	2	3

Once you have gathered your materials, you are ready to begin

WORKSHOP BEGINS

The instructions are presented as a verbatim script progressing through the various workshop stages. The facilitator should read all information provided. Each component is an integral part of the complete program so do not read ahead or skip any exercises; you will not benefit as much if you do. Simply read the step-by-step instructions and complete each exercise as presented.

If some people have not read this book, or for a reminder, read the following Workshop Objective and Review of terms.

Workshop Objectives and Review of Terms

This workshop includes the necessary tools to maximize the satisfaction of your needs in re-tirement. You will learn how to:

- Identify your needs and skills
- Evaluate and possibly improve current re-tirement plans
- Create new plans (if necessary)
- Guide your re-tirement career so it will be worthwhile and enjoyable.

Life Goal Planning is based on the following facts.

- The reason we enjoy any activity is because it satisfies our needs and gives us the opportunity to use our skills. For example, work can satisfy the need for money, friendships, routine, stimulation, power, and so on.
- When you re-tire, your needs and skills met by work will no longer be satisfied.
- The same need can be satisfied by a completely different activity at a different life stage.
- Therefore, the key to re-tirement happiness is to maximize needs satisfaction, especially those lost from work.

The Road Map to Retirement Happiness includes the following terms.

- The territory of your road map is a career earned from and following work
- Your objective or destination in re-tirement is to satisfy your needs, especially those lost from work
- Your route to reach your destination includes the activities you plan to or are pursuing in re-tirement.
- Your method of travel is based on your financial circumstances.

The Workshop is divided into 5 stages or steps as follows:

1. List Retirement Plans
2. Create Needs and Skills List
3. Evaluate Retirement Plans
4. How to Develop New Plans
5. Guide Your Re-tirement Career

1) List Your Re-tirement Plans

List the activities that you plan to or would like to pursue when you re-tire on the sheet headed "Re-tirement Plans". If you are re-tired, write your currents pursuits. If your main occupation is homemaking, think about what you plan to do when your spouse re-tires. It doesn't matter if your plans are concrete or vague. Soon you will evaluate your plans and you will clarify your thinking by writing them down. Your plans include your 'proposed' route in re-tirement.

{Pause}

Each person should read his or her plans to the group; this sharing could prove to be quite interesting.

2) Create Your Needs and Skills List

Given that the key to re-tirement happiness (your objective or destination in re-tirement) is to satisfy your needs and skills, the first thing you must do is identify them. You can create your Needs and Skills List by answering six simple questions. Write your answers, one per line, on your "Activity Evaluation List" under the heading "Needs & Skills". Do not duplicate answers or items. Give some thought to your answer.

{Allow about 5 minutes per question to write the answers}

Question #1: Needs Satisfied by Work.

If you are not already re-tired, imagine you are re-tiring tomorrow: What are the main things you will miss, or do miss, from work? (For example you might miss friendships, routine, challenge, money, stimulation and so on). Forget about the things you are happy to give up (like morning traffic).

The things you will miss from work are in fact your needs satisfied by work and the key to re-tirement happiness is based in part on replacing these needs.

{Pause}

Question #2: Work Skills

Now list the skills you have developed through work, one per line, starting on the next available line. These can be job specific such as writing, teaching, computer skills, etc.; but you are encouraged to include more general or transferable skills such as being good with people, time management, leadership, organizational skills, and so on.

Sometimes we lose sight of our skills or take them for granted because they are second nature to us and our colleagues have similar skills. So imagine you had to hire the person to fill your job after you re-tire and list the skills you would look for in your replacement.

It is important to identify your work skills because part of the reason we enjoy certain activities is they give us the opportunity to use our skills. Also, because skills are transferable, they may be applied to a different activity in retirement.

{Pause}

Question #3: Needs Satisfied by Current Leisure

On the next available line, list a current leisure activity, for example going to a movie, and below list several reasons (one reason per line) why you enjoy it. Continue with other leisure activities you enjoy. If you find that a reason for enjoying an activity is already on your list do not add the same reason twice.

Your reasons for enjoying leisure are in fact your needs satisfied by leisure. As such they can provide important clues to re-tirement happiness.

{Pause}

Question #4: Needs Satisfied by Past Leisure

On the next available line list a leisure activity from the past when you were a kid or before you started working full-time, and then list your reasons (one reason per line) for enjoying that activity.

Thinking about leisure in the past and why you enjoyed it may identify additional needs. Spend some time with this exercise as it can help identify important needs we may have forgotten about. Again, do not duplicate activities or reasons for enjoying past leisure if they are already on your list.

{Pause}

Question #5: Leisure Skills

Now put modesty aside and list the things you are good at that are not already on your list. For example, include what others have said you are good at whether or not these skills seem trivial to you.

Skills might be specific such as carpentry, painting, gardening, cooking, or more general such as being good with children, a good listener, or a good letter writer. As with all of the clues on your Needs and Skills List, you never know which will prove to be the most insightful so don't think, "Big deal, anybody could be good at that," simply put down everything you can think of.

{Pause}

Question #6: Re-tirement Needs

Finally, list the things you look forward to when you no longer have to work. Think about and complete the following statement, "When I re-tire I am looking forward to....". Your list may include things like freedom, sleeping-in, travel, more time with my spouse/friends, no hassles, and so on. Again, only include those things that are not already on your Needs and Skills List. If you are re-tired, list anything else you enjoy about re-tirement.

{Pause}

This completes Step 2 and your Needs and Skills List. It will look something like the following example.

Activity Evaluation List

Needs & Skills	1	2	3
money			
friendships			
routine			
stimulation			
time management			
organized			
golf			
challenge			
exercise			

Before continuing with the next exercise, look at the value of what you have created. Review your complete list and ask yourself: If all the important items on my list were met in re-tirement, would my re-tirement be worthwhile and enjoyable?

I suspect your answer is 'yes'.

You now possess something of value most re-tirees do not have. You know your destination or where you are heading in re-tirement. You know your re-tirement will be worthwhile and enjoyable if it satisfies the needs and skills on your list. Think of your Needs and Skills List as a wish list or a measuring rod to evaluate your re-tirement plans. It will also prove invaluable should you want to come up with new ideas for re-tirement.

3) Evaluate Your Re-tirement Plans

One thing is certain - you won't know what your re-tirement will be like until you experience it. But you can objectively evaluate your re-tirement plans by assessing whether or not they are likely to satisfy your needs.

To do this, compare the re-tirement plans you listed in Step 1 with your Needs and Skills List. For each item on your Needs and Skills List, ask yourself: "Considering my re-tirement plans, will this item be met to my satisfaction?" You can answer yes (Y), no (N), or I'm not sure (?) if you have to wait until you re-tire. If you are re-tired, your evaluation will be based on your current pursuits and you will have no question marks. Be honest with yourself and do not skip any items.

You can feel fairly confident your re-tirement will be worthwhile and enjoyable if most of your important needs and skills will be met when you re-tire. However, if you identified needs or skills that are important to you and that you do not think will be met given your plans, you should consider how you can improve your plans so that particular need or skill will be met.

Activity Evaluation List

Needs & Skills	1	2	3
money	Y		
friendships	Y		
routine	N		
stimulation	?		
time management	Y		
organized	Y		
golf	Y		
challenge	N		
exercise	Y		

You can evaluate different re-tirement plan scenarios by using the separate columns on your Activity Evaluation List sheet (columns noted 1, 2, 3). Comparing the results may make it obvious which plan is likely to satisfy more of your needs and skills, and hence be more worthwhile and enjoyable.

4) How To Develop New (or Revise) Plans

Your plans may look like they will satisfy all of your needs and skills, however conditions could change or your plans may lose their appeal after the initial euphoria of the "honeymoon" stage wears off. At any time you may feel something is missing from your current re-tirement and you may be looking for new interests. It is therefore important to learn how to create new plans.

Finding the perfect re-tirement activities may take some time; they will not likely fall into your lap. Surprisingly for many people, what you end up doing in re-tirement may never have entered your mind when you first contemplated re-tirement. The best way to start is through a group brainstorming session. The purpose of the brainstorming session is to come up with as many ideas as possible to build on for your re-tirement career.

Brainstorming Re-tirement Plans

The objective of the brainstorming session is for group members to make re-tirement suggestions to each other. Imagine a group of four people, Dave, Diane, Les and Janice.

- Each group member takes a turn reading their complete Needs and Skills List to the group. Dave starts and reads his Needs and Skills List aloud.
- The others listen carefully and write down what they consider to be Dave's important needs and skills on their sheet headed "Brainstorming Notes".
- Each group member must suggest at least one activity for the reader in re-tirement based on his or her brainstorming notes. They may tie together two or three of Dave's needs or skills into a single activity. For example, if Dave mentioned travel, gardening, good organizer, and enjoying the people he works with, Janice might suggest he organize a group to tour gardens in England. Les might suggest that he get a job at a garden center, and so on.

- When a suggestion is made, and this is very important, Dave (the reader) must write the suggestion as given on his sheet headed "Suggestions Received". He should not evaluate or discuss the suggestion at this point; he should simply write it down as given.

- When receiving suggestions, do not judge or eliminate a suggestion because it does not appeal to you or you don't think you can do it.

- At the same time, when each person makes a suggestion they **must** write the suggestion they gave to Dave on their sheet headed "Suggestions Given". When making a suggestion, do not ask questions, elaborate on or justify your suggestion. For now you simply give and receive as many suggestions as possible.

When making suggestions, keep the discussion to a minimum and keep in mind you are not making suggestions for yourself, you are helping a group member. Make any suggestion you think might satisfy the reader's needs and skills when he or she re-tires. Try to come up with realistic suggestions, but remember - anything goes, be creative, and use lateral thinking.

Try to allot approximately 6-minutes for each person to read their list and receive suggestions. With a group of 4 people, each person will end up with at least 6 suggestions — 3 on the "Suggestions Received" sheet and 3 on the "Suggestions Given" sheet. The facilitator should watch the time and ensure that both the person who receives and gives a suggestion writes it on the appropriate sheet.

Hopefully you will come up with several suggestions for each person in your group. They do not have to be perfect. This is just a starting point. Every suggestion has the potential of providing you with a clue to enhance your enjoyment in re-tirement.

Brainstorming On Your Own

If you are on your own, follow the instructions for the group brainstorming above, but pretend the Needs and Skills List you developed earlier belongs to someone else. Put aside for the moment your likes, dislikes, abilities, and limitations. Try to be totally removed and objective and identify the key needs and skills. Then brainstorm a few suggestions for re-tirement that you think will satisfy those needs and skills.

Evaluate Re-tirement Career Suggestions

You have now received several suggestions to work with. And here is a secret that may reveal additional items for your Needs and Skills List, and in turn help you find the perfect re-tirement. Examine your list of "Suggestions Given" What do you see?

{Pause}

In all likelihood you see some suggestions that appeal to you. The reason for this is when you are making a suggestion to someone else, in essence you are saying, "If I had your interests and skills, this is what I would do."

Do you see any patterns in the suggestions you made for others? Did you make several suggestions that involved, say, starting a business, teaching, helping others, or joining something? If you see a pattern among the suggestions you made, or any new words that appeal to you, you have identified additional needs or skills to add to your list.

Now review your "Suggestions Received" list. Identify part or all suggestions that appeal to you and add them to your Needs and Skills list, if they are not already there.

{Pause}

Improving Current Plans

A visualization exercise may also help to improve your plans by revealing additional needs or skills. Assume you have several appealing suggestions, but none that appear perfect. Choose the suggestion that appeals to you the most, even if it seems a bit unrealistic. Imagine you are involved in that activity and ask yourself what you would enjoy about that activity or what needs and skills that activity would satisfy. If you identify reasons for enjoying that activity that are not already on your Needs and Skills List, add them.

Then, examine your expanded Needs and Skills list and ask yourself if these additional items will be met given your re-tirement plans. If not, and if they are important to you, ask yourself how you can improve your plans so that some of these new needs or skills will be met. Although you may be visualizing a somewhat unrealistic activity, it can reveal additional needs that may be satisfied through a more realistic activity.

{Pause}

The steps outlined above can be initiated before you re-tire, but you may have to wait until after you re-tire to see if your plans satisfy your needs and skills. If you are ever looking for something new, select the activity from the suggestions given or received that appeals to you most. You never know where pursuing this activity can lead. Continue to brainstorm and evaluate your activities based on your Needs and Skills List to improve the original suggestions. The group may be able to help brainstorm improvements. Simply share the activity with the group along with what does and does not appeal about that activity. {Pause}

When this process is taken as far as it can go, you will have one or more suggestions that are good but perhaps not perfect. Don't worry; you can perfect your plans when you re-tire. This takes us to the final step.

5) Experience Your Re-tirement Career

You have now identified your needs and skills, and can use this list to evaluate future plans and create new ideas. This will allow you to steer the course of your re-tirement through pursuing activities that will enable you to satisfy your needs.

Sailing a boat is a good analogy of how your re-tirement career will develop and progress. When you go sailing, you know your destination. What you don't know for certain is the route you will take - more than likely you have to tack or zigzag to reach your destination. In other words, you discover your route, en route.

More than likely you will have to 'tack' or experience several activities before you satisfy all your important needs and skills on your list and thereby reach your re-tirement destination.

If you find that something is missing in your re-tirement, go back to your Needs and Skills List. Evaluate each item on your list against your current experience. If you identify an important item(s) is missing, brainstorm a new plan. The important point is you are now basing your brainstorming on your experience with your first re-tirement plan, say taking a locum position in a new location, and therefore you may come up with something quite new that you might not have thought of before you took on the locum in the new location. If your next plan is still not perfect, continue the process until you reach your destination.

If you continue to use the process outlined in this workshop, eventually you will end up with re-tirement activities that are perfect for you.